THE

2001 CHARLTON
COIN GUIDE

40TH EDITION

Dealer's Buying Prices For
Canadian, Newfoundland and Maritime Coinage,
Canadian Medals, Tokens and Paper Money,
United States and World Gold Coinage

W. K. Cross
Publisher

The Charlton Press
Toronto, Ontario Palm Harbor, Florida

Canadian Cataloguing in Publication Data

The National Library of Canada has catalogued this publication as follows:

Charlton, J. E., 1911
    Charlton coin guide

18th ed. (1978)-
Continues: Charlton, J. E. 1911-   Coin guide of Canadian, Newfoundland and Maritime coinage.
ISSN 0706-0459
ISBN 0-88968-236-4 (40th ed.)

1. Coins, Canadian - Periodicals. 2. Coins - Prices - Periodicals. I. Title.

CJ1864.C5114   737.4' 9'71   C79-030323-X

**Printed in Canada
in the Province of Ontario**

The Charlton Press

**2040 Yonge Street, Suite 208, Toronto, Ontario. M4S 1Z9
Tel: (416) 488-1418 Fax: (416) 488-4656
Tel: (800) 442-6042 Fax: (800) 442-1542
www.charltonpress.comm e-mail Chpress@charltonpress.com**

CONTENTS

INDEX OF DEALERS

INTRODUCTION

It is more difficult to obtain old coins in circulation, much more so than it was twenty-five years go. For the most part silver no longer circulates, since its bullion value now exceeds its face alue. Generally speaking, the only pre-1968 coins in circulation are one-cent and five-cent ieces, and these seldom pre-date 1953. Older coins must now be purchased through dealers.

BUYING AND SELLING PRICES

Buying prices are what dealers pay for coins. Selling prices are what dealers charge for coins. ienerally, dealers will pay 40% to 60% of their selling price. It should be remembered all ealers will pay according to their needs. They will pay well for what they need immediately, ut for those coins for which there is no demand, even if they have a high retail value, they ill offer substantially less.

The prices shown in this book represent averages or estimates of buying prices and should erve as a guide in negotiating fair prices when buying or selling. Also a clearer idea of which oins are in demand by collectors and dealers can be developed by studying the guide.

Coins should not be mailed for appraisal unless a written response to an inquiry is received om the dealer. If coins are mailed, then they should be sent by registered mail, insured, ccompanied by a list of the coins sent, with a complete return address and return postage.

HANDLING AND CLEANING COINS

Coins should be handled by the edges only. Avoid touching the surfaces. Many collectors ave found too late that fingerprints cannot be removed from coins or other metal valuables. roof and specimen quality coins must be handled with extra care since their high lustre is ery fragile.

Inevitably, the question of whether to clean coins or not will arise. Probably the best course follow is, when in doubt don't, until you have contacted an experienced collector or dealer. The tarnish on silver coins can be removed, but it will not necessarily raise the value. If the rnish is very thick, then its removal could leave the coin looking much worse.

Nickel coins seldom require cleaning, and only soap and water are safe since nickel is a fairly ctive metal. Copper and bronze should not be cleaned by anyone who is not knowledgeable the chemical properties of these metals and their alloys.

Whatever the metal, abrasives must never be used. There are many polishes on the market hich are designed for silverware, copper and brass. These must not be used with coins. The sults are disastrous.

HANDLING AND CLEANING PAPER MONEY

nexperienced collectors should always use great care when handling notes. Notes should e handled as little as possible, since oil and perspiration from one's skin can damage and evalue a note. Care should be taken to ensure that unfolded or uncreased notes remain so, d that even marginal tears or abrasions are avoided. Under no circumstances should one ver wash or otherwise try to clean a note since it is likely that the note's value will be nsiderably reduced. The same is true for ironing or pressing. It should be avoided.

MINT MARKS

A mint mark is a letter stamped on a coin to designate the mint that produced the coins. Canadian decimal coinage issued prior to 1908 was struck at either the Tower Mint, London, which case it has no mint mark, or at the Heaton Mint in Birmingham. The Birmingham coins ave a small "H" as a mint mark. Since 1908 all Canadian coins have been struck at the Ottawa Winnipeg Mints, with no mint marks, except the Canadian sovereigns which were identified a small "C" above the date and a "W" when struck at Winnipeg.

Newfoundland's coinage was struck at either London, Birmingham, or Ottawa. The Tower int coins had no marks, the Birmingham coins had an "H," and the Ottawa coins had a "C," xcept for the 1940 and 1942 cent pieces.

The coinage of New Brunswick and Nova Scotia had no mint marks because it was struck the Tower Mint. Prince Edward Island's coinage was struck at Birmingham, but no mint ark was used because the dies were supplied by the Tower Mint.

COINS OF CANADA

NOVA SCOTIA

VICTORIA 1861 - 1864

Date and Denomination	Buying Price
1861 half cent	4.00
1864 half cent	4.00
1861 one cent	2.00
1862 one cent	20.00
1864 one cent	2.00

PRINCE EDWARD ISLAND

VICTORIA 1871

Date and Denomination	Buying Price
1871 one cent	1.00

NEW BRUNSWICK

VICTORIA 1861 - 1864

Date and Denomination	Buying Price
1861 half cent	50.00
1861 one cent	1.25
1864 one cent	1.25
1862 five cents	30.00
1864 five cents	30.00
1862 ten cents	30.00
1864 ten cents	30.00
1862 twenty cents	20.00
1864 twenty cents	20.00

IMPORTANT: Buying prices are listed for coins graded VG or better. Bent, damaged or badly worn coins are not collectable and bring no premium value.

7

NEWFOUNDLAND

LARGE CENTS

Wide O   Narrow O

VICTORIA 1865 - 1896

Date and Mint Mark	Description	Buying Price
1865		2.00
1872H		2.00
1873		2.00
1876H		2.00
1880	Wide O	2.00
1880	Narrow O	100.00
1885		20.00
1888		17.50
1890		2.00
1894		2.00
1896		2.00

EDWARD VII 1904 - 1909

Date and Mint Mark	Buying Price
1904H	5.00
1907	1.50
1909	1.50

GEORGE V 1913 - 1936

Date and Mint Mark	Buyi Pri
1913	.
1917C	.
1919C	.
1920C	.
1929	.
1936	.

SMALL CENTS

GEORGE VI 1938 - 1948

Date and Mint Mark	Description	Buyi Pri
1938		.
1940		.
1940	Re-engraved Date	15.
1941C		.
1942		.
1943C		.
1944C		.
1947C		.

FIVE CENTS

VICTORIA 1865 - 1896

Date and Mint Mark	Buyi Pri
1865	25.
1870	40.
1872H	25.
1873	50.
1873H	800.
1876H	70.
1880	35.

Date and Mint Mark	Buying Price
881	20.00
882H	18.00
885	95.00
888	30.00
890	6.00
894	6.00
896	4.00

EDWARD VII 1903 - 1908

Date and Mint Mark	Buying Price
903	2.00
904H	1.50
908	1.50

GEORGE V 1912 - 1929

Date and Mint Mark	Buying Price
912	.75
917C	.75
919C	3.00
929	.75

GEORGE VI 1938 - 1947

Date and Mint Mark	Buying Price
938	.75
940C	.75
941C	.75
942C	.75
943C	.75
944C	.75
945C	.75
946C	200.00
947C	.75

TEN CENTS

VICTORIA 1865 - 1896

Date and Mint Mark	Buying Price
1865	15.00
1870	150.00
1872H	15.00
1873	20.00
1876H	20.00
1880	25.00
1882H	15.00
1885	50.00
1888	15.00
1890	4.00
1894	4.00
1896	4.00

EDWARD VII 1903 - 1904

Date and Mint Mark	Buying Price
1903	3.00
1904H	2.00

GEORGE V 1912 -1919

Date and Mint Mark	Buying Price
1912	.50
1917C	.50
1919C	2.00

IMPORTANT: Buying prices are listed for coins graded VG or better. Bent, damaged or badly worn coins are not collectable and bring no premium value.

9

GEORGE VI 1938 - 1947

Date and Mint Mark	Buying Price
1938	.45
1940	.45
1941C	.45
1942C	.45
1943C	.45
1944C	.45
1945C	.45
1946C	1.00
1947C	.75

EDWARD VII 1904

Date and Mint Mark	Buying Price
1904H	5.0

TWENTY CENTS

GEORGE V 1912

Date and Mint Mark	Buying Price
1912	1.0

TWENTY-FIVE CENTS

VICTORIA 1865 - 1900

Date and Mint Mark	Buying Price
1865	10.00
1870	15.00
1872H	7.00
1873	8.00
1876H	15.00
1880	15.00
1881	5.00
1882H	5.00
1885	7.00
1888	5.00
1890	4.00
1894	4.00
1896	4.00
1899	3.00
1900	3.00

GEORGE V 1917 - 1919

Date and Mint Mark	Buying Price
1917C	1.5
1919C	1.5

IMPORTANT: Mint marks are a letter stamped on a coin to designate the mint that produced the coin. The Canadian Mint used the letter "C" or "W," while the Heaton Mint in England used the letter "H."

IMPORTANT: Buying prices are listed for coins graded VG or better. Bent, damaged or badly worn coins are not collectable and bring no premium.

FIFTY CENTS

VICTORIA 1870 - 1900

Date and Mint Mark	Buying Price
1870	12.00
1872H	12.00
1873	35.00
1874	20.00
1876H	20.00
1880	20.00
1881	15.00
1882H	7.00
1885	8.00
1888	20.00
1894	3.00
1896	3.00
1898	3.00
1899	3.00
1900	3.00

GEORGE V 1911 - 1919

Date and Mint Mark	Buying Price
1911	2.25
1917C	2.25
1918C	2.25
1919C	2.25

TWO DOLLARS GOLD

VICTORIA 1865 - 1888

Date and Mint Mark	Buying Price
1865	175.00
1870	165.00
1872	250.00
1880	1,000.00
1881	135.00
1882H	135.00
1885	135.00
1888	135.00

EDWARD VII 1904 - 1909

Date and Mint Mark	Buying Price
1904H	3.00
1907	3.00
1908	3.00
1909	3.00

PROVINCE OF CANADA

LARGE CENTS

Wide 9 over 8   Narrow 9

VICTORIA 1858 - 1859

Date and Mint Mark	Description	Buying Price
1858		30.00
1859		1.00
1859	W/9 over 8	20.00

FIVE CENTS

Large date   Small date

VICTORIA 1858

Date and Mint Mark	Description	Buying Price
1858	Small Date	13.00
1858	Large Date	120.00

TEN CENTS

VICTORIA 1858

Date and Mint Mark	Buying Price
1858	15.0

TWENTY CENTS

VICTORIA 1858

Date and Mint Mark	Buying Price
1858	50.0

IMPORTANT: Buying prices are listed for coins graded VG or better. Bent, damaged or badly worn coins are not collectable and bring no premium value.

IMPORTANT: The buying prices f silver coins are based on their intrins value. All issues from 1902 to 1968 a priced at the market value for $7.5 (Can. funds) silver. Conditions play a important part in the buying price f coins between 1902 and 1936. Higher lower silver prices will change the liste values.

12

CANADA

LARGE CENTS

EDWARD VII 1902 - 1910

Date and Mint Mark	Buying Price
1902	.75
1903	.75
1904	.75
1905	.75
1906	.75
1907	.75
1907H	5.00
1908	.75
1909	.75
1910	.75

Large Date, Large Leaves

Small Date, Small Leaves

VICTORIA 1876 - 1901

Date and Mint Mark	Description	Buying Price
1876H		1.25
1881H		1.25
1882H		1.25
1884		1.25
1886		1.25
1887		1.25
1888		1.25
1890H		4.00
1891	Large Leaves, Large Date	4.00
1891	Large Leaves, Small Date	40.00
1891	Small Leaves, Small Date	30.00
1892		1.25
1893		1.25
1894		1.25
1895		1.25
1896		1.25
1897		1.25
1898H		1.25
1899		1.25
1900		1.25
1900H		1.25
1901		1.25

GEORGE V 1911 - 1920

Date and Mint Mark	Buying Price
1911	.20
1912	.20
1913	.20
1914	.20
1915	.20
1916	.20
1917	.20
1918	.20
1919	.20
1920	.20

Large cents were not issued for the years omitted in this listing.

IMPORTANT: Buying prices are listed for coins graded VG or better. Bent, damaged or badly worn coins are not collectable and bring no premium value.

SMALL CENTS

GEORGE V 1920 - 1936

Date and Mint Mark	Buying Price
1920 to 1921	.05
1922	7.00
1923	12.00
1924	3.50
1925	10.00
1926	1.50
1927 to 1929	.05
1930	.30
1931	.10
1932 to 1936	.05

1947 Maple Leaf

GEORGE VI 1937 - 1947

Date and Mint Mark	Description	Buying Price
1937 to 1947		.01
1947	Maple Leaf	.01

GEORGE VI 1948 - 1952

Date and Mint Mark	Description	Buying Price
1948	Without "ET IND:IMP"	.01
1949 to 1952		.01

No should fold   Shoulder Fold

ELIZABETH II 1953 - 1964

Date and Mint Mark	Description	Buying Price
1953	NSF	.0
1953	SF	.5
1954	NSF	100.0
1954	SF	.0
1955	NSF	50.0
1955	SF	.0
1956 to 1964		.0

Mature Head-Round   Centennial

ELIZABETH ii 1965 - 1981

Date and Mint Mark	Description	Buying Price
1965 to 1966		.0
1967	Centennial	.0
1968 to 1981		.0

Mature Head 12-sided

ELIZABETH II 1982 - 1989

Date and Mint Mark	Description	Buying Price
1982 to 1989		.0

Double Date

FIVE CENTS SILVER

𝟙 𝟡 𝟘 𝟘   𝟙 𝟡 𝟘 𝟘
1900 Small Date   1900 Large Date

𝟙 𝟠 𝟟 𝟜   𝟙 𝟠 𝟟 𝟜
Plain 4   Crosslet 4

ELIZABETH II 1990 to 1996

Date and Mint Mark	Description	Buying Price
1990 to 1991		.01
1992	Double Date	.01
1993 to 1996		.01

ELIZABETH II 1997 to 2001

Date and Mint Mark	Buying Price
1997 to 2001	.01

VICTORIA 1870 - 1901

Date and Mint Mark	Description	Buying Price
1870		8.00
1871		8.00
1872H		8.00
1874H	Plain 4	15.00
1874H	Crosslet 4	9.00
1875H	Large Date	100.00
1875H	Small Date	75.00
1880H		4.00
1881H		6.00
1882H		7.00
1883H		15.00
1884		95.00
1885		7.00
1886		7.00
1887		14.00
1888		4.00
1889		15.00
1890H		4.00
1891		4.00
1892		4.00
1893		4.00
1894		14.00
1896		4.00
1897		4.00
1898		7.00
1899		4.00
1900	Large Date	15.00
1900	Small Date	4.00
1901		4.00

Small H   Large H

FIVE CENTS NICKEL

Near 6   Far 6

EDWARD VII 1902 - 1910

Date and Mint Mark	Description	Buying Price
1902	Plain	1.00
1902	Large H	12.50
1902	Small H	4.00
1903		2.00
1903H		1.50
1904		1.50
1905		1.50
1906		1.50
1907		1.50
1908		3.00
1909		1.50
1910		1.50

GEORGE V 1922 - 1936

Date and Mint Mark	Description	Buying Price
1922 to 1924		.0˙
1925		22.0●
1926	Near 6	1.0●
1926	Far 6	50.0●
1927 to 1936		.0˙

Tombac Beaver   Tombac "V"

GEORGE V 1911 - 1921

Date and Mint Mark	Buying Price
1911	.75
1912	.75
1913	.75
1914	.75
1915	5.00
1916	.75
1917	.75
1918	.75
1919	.75
1920	.75
1921	1,5
00.00	

1947 Maple Leaf

GEORGE VI 1937 - 1952

Date and Mint Mark	Description	Buying Price
1937	Dot	.0▪
1938 to 1941		.0▪
1942	Nickel	.0▪
1942	Tombac Beaver	.1▪
1943	Tombac V	.0˙
1944 to 1945	Steel V	.1●
1946 to 1947		.0▪
1947	Maple Leaf	.0▪

Geo. VI Obverse

Beaver

1951 High Relief

1951 Comm.

Centennial

EORGE VI 1948 - 1952

te and nt Mark	Description	Buying Price
48	Without "ET IND:IMP"	.05
49 to 1951		.05
51	Commemorative	.05
51	High Relief	200.00
52		.05

ELIABETH II 1965 - 1989

Date and Mint Mark	Description	Buying Price
1965 to 1966		.05
1967	Centennial	.05
1968 to 1989		.05

IZABETH II 1953 - 1962

te and nt Mark	Buying Price
53 to 1962	.05

Double Date

IZABETH II 1963 - 1964

te and nt Mark	Buying Price
63 to 1964	.05

ELIZABETH II 1990 - 2000

Date and Mint Mark	Description	Buying Price
1990 to 1991		.05
1992	Double Date	.05
1999 to 2001		.05

TEN CENTS

Flat Top 3   Round Top 3

VICTORIA 1870 -1901

Date and Mint Mark	Description	Buying Price
1870		15.00
1871		20.00
1871H		20.00
1872H		75.00
1874H		10.00
1875H		175.00
1880H		10.00
1881H		10.00
1882H		10.00
1883H		30.00
1884		150.00
1885		20.00
1886		15.00
1887		20.00
1888		8.00
1889		375.00
1890H		10.00
1891		10.00
1892		10.00
1893	Flat Top 3	8.00
1893	Round Top 3	400.00
1894		15.00
1896		8.00
1898		8.00
1899		8.00
1900		7.00
1901		7.00

EDWARD VII 1902 - 1910

Date and Mint Mark	Buying Price
1902	4.0
1902H	3.0
1903	5.0
1903H	3.0
1904	4.0
1905	3.0
1906	4.0
1907	4.0
1908	4.0
1909	4.0
1910	3.0

Small Leaves   Broad Leaves

GEORGE V 1911 - 1936

Date and Mint Mark	Description	Buying Price
1911		4.0
1912		.5
1913	Broad Leaves	85.0
1913	Small Leaves	.5
1914 to 1936		.5

GEORGE VI 1937 - 1947

Date and Mint Mark	Description	Buying Price
1937 to 1947		.3
1947	Maple Leaf	.3

EORGE VI 1948 - 1952

ate and Int Mark	Description	Buying Price
)48	Without "ET IND"IMP"	.50
)49 to 1952		.30

LIZABETH II 1953 - 1964

ate and Int Mark	Buying Price
)53 to 1964	.30

Centennial

1969 Small Date   1969 Large Date

.IZABETH II 1965 - 1989

te and nt Mark	Description	Buying Price
)65 to 1966		.30
)67	Centennial	.25
)68	.500 Fine Silver	.30
)68	Nickel	.10
)69	Large Date	6,500.00
)69	Small Date	.10
)70 to 1989		.10

Double Date

ELIZABETH 1990 - 2001

Date and Mint Mark	Description	Buying Price
1990 to 1991		.10
1992	Double Date	.10
1993 to 2001		.10

19

TWENTY-FIVE CENTS

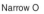

Narrow O	Wide O

VICTORIA 1870 - 1901

Date and Mint Mark	Description	Buying Price
1870		10.00
1871		15.00
1871H		15.00
1872H		7.00
1874H		7.00
1875H		300.00
1880H	Narrow O	40.00
1880H	Wide O	100.00
1881H		12.00
1882H		12.00
1883H		10.00
1885		100.00
1886		12.00
1887		85.00
1888		15.00
1889		100.00
1890H		15.00
1891		45.00
1892		9.00
1893		85.00
1894		12.00
1899		7.00
1900		7.00
1901		7.00

EDWARD VII 1902 - 1910

Date and Mint Mark	Buying Price
1902	4.0
1902H	4.0
1903	6.0
1904	10.0
1905	5.0
1906	6.0
1907	4.0
1908	6.0
1909	4.0
1910	4.0

GEORGE V 1911- 1936

Date and Mint Mark	Description	Buying Price
1911		5.0
1912 to 1914		2.0
1915		8.0
1916 to 1920		2.0
1921		6.0
1927		15.0
1928 to 1936		2.0
1936	Dot	20.0

GEORGE VI 1937 - 1947

Date and Mint Mark	Description	Buying Price
1937 to 1947		.
1947	Maple Leaf	.

GEORGE VI 1948 - 1952

Date and Mint Mark	Descripton	Buying Price
1948	Without "ET IND:IMP"	.75
1949 to 1952		.75

ELIZABETH II 1953 - 1964

Date and Mint Mark	Description	Buying Price
1953	Large Date	.75
1953	Small Date	.75
1954 to 1964		.75

Centennial

ELIZABETH II 1965 - 1972

Date and Mint Mark	Description	Buying Price
1965 to 1966		.75
1967	Centennial	.60
1968	.500 Fine Silver	.45
1968 to 1972	Nickel	.25

1973 Small Bust
120 Obverse Beads
Far from Rim

1973 Large Bust
132 Obverse Beads
Near Rim

1974/89 Mature Head
Small Beads

Caribou.

RCMP

ELIZABETH II 1973 - 1989

Date and Mint Mark	Description	Buying Price
1973	Small Bust	.2
1973	Large Bust	20.0
1974 to 1989		.2

ELIZABETH II 1990 - 1991

Date and Mint Mark	Buying Price
1990	.2
1991	1.0

CANADA 125 ANNIVERSARY

Issued in 1992 to commemorate Canada's 125th birthday. The twelve different quarters present images from the ten provinces and two territories. The composition is nickel.

Common Obverse

New Brunswick

Northwest Territories

Newfoundland

Manitoba

Yukon

Alberta

Prince Edward Island

Ontario

Nova Scotia

Quebec

Saskatchewan

British Columbia

ELIZABETH II 1992

Date and Mint Mark	Description	Buying Price
1992	New Brunswick	.25
1992	Northwest Territories	.25
1992	Newfoundland	.25
1992	Manitoba	.25
1992	Yukon	.25
1992	Alberta	.25
1992	Prince Edward Island	.25
1992	Ontario	.25
1992	Nova Scotia	.25
1992	Quebec	.25
1992	Saskatchewan	.25
1992	British Columbia	.25
1992	Double Date	2.00

Note: 1992 Caribou double date quarters found only in RCM sets.

ELIZABETH II 1993 - 2001

Date and Mint Mark	Description	Buying Price
1993 to 1996		.25
1997	1997 to 2000	2.00
1998	Caribou quarters found	2.00
1999	only in R.C.M. Sets	2.00
2000		2.00
2001		.25

1999 MILLENNIUM QUARTERS

Issued to start the Millennium celebration, the following twelve quarters were released one per month during 1999. The obverse is as the 1993 issue.

Common Obverse

January

February

March

April

May

June

July

August

September

October

November

December

ELIZABETH 1999

Date and Mint Mark	Description	Buying Price
1999	January	.
1999	February	.
1999	March	.
1999	April	.
1999	May	.
1999	June	.
1999	July	.
1999	August	.
1999	September	.
1999	October	.
1999	November	.
1999	December	.

Queen Elizabeth
Caribou Reverse

September

November

Date and Mint Mark	Description	Buying Price
1999	September Mule	50.
1999	November Mule	50.

2000 MILLENNIUM QUARTERS

his set of twelve is the final issue of enty-five cent coins for the Millennium lebration.

September   October

Common Obverse

November   December

January   February

Elizabeth 2000

Date and Mint Mark	Description	Buying Price
2000	January, Pride	1.00
2000	February, Ingenuity	1.00
2000	March, Achievement	1.00
2000	April, Health	1.00
2000	May, Natural Legacy	1.00
2000	June, Harmony	1.00
2000	July, Celebration	1.00
2000	August, Family	1.00
2000	September, Wisdom	1.00
2000	October. Creativity	1.00
2000	November, Freedom	1.00
2000	December, Community	1.00

March   April

2000 Millennium Medallion

May   June

2000 Error Millennium Medallion

July   August

Date and Mint Mark	Description	Buying Price
2000	Queen Elizabeth Mule with Medallion reverse	1,000.00

25

FIFTY CENTS

L.C.W.	No L.C.W.

VICTORIA 1870 - 1901

Date and Mint Mark	Description	Buying Price
1870	Without L.C.W.	450.00
1870	With L.C.W.	40.00
1871		55.00
1871H		85.00
1872H		40.00
1881H		40.00
1888		125.00
1890H		650.00
1892		45.00
1894		300.00
1898		40.00
1899		90.00
1900		25.00
1901		25.00

GEORGE V 1911 - 1936

Date and Mint Mark	Buying Price
1911 to 1920	3.
1921*	9,000.
1929	3.
1931	8.
1932	40.
1934	10.
1936	10.

*Majority were melted down. Approximate 75 are known. Beware of altered date.

Straight "7" No Maple Leaf	Curved "7" No Maple Leaf
Staight "7" With Maple Leaf	Curved "7" With Maple Leaf

EDWARD VII 1902 - 1910

Date and Mint Mark	Buying Price
1902	9.00
1903H	15.00
1904	75.00
1905	75.00
1906	13.00
1907	9.00
1908	5.00
1909	5.00
1910	5.00

GEORGE VI 1937 - 1947

Date and Mint Mark	Description	Buying Price
1937 to 1946		1.
1947	Straight "7"	1.
1947	Curved "7"	1.
1947	M.L., Straight "7"	12.
1947	M.L., Curved "7"	600.

ORGE VI 1948 - 1952

e and t Mark	Description	Buying Price
8	Without "ET IND:IMP"	30.00
9 to 1952		1.50

No shoulder fold   Shoulder fold

Small date   Large date

ZABETH II 1953 to 1964

e and t Mark	Description	Buying Price
3	SD, NSF	1.50
3	LD, NSF	3.00
3	LD, SF	1.50
4 to 1964		1.50

ELIZABETH II 1965 - 1967

Date and Mint Mark	Description	Buying Price
1965 to 1966		1.50
1967	Centennial	1.50

ELIZABETH II 1968 - 1989

Date and Mint Mark		Buying Price
1968 to 1989		.50

ELIZABETH II 1990 - 2001

Date and Mint Mark	Description	Buying Price
1990 to 1991		.50
1992	Double date	.50
1993 to 1995		.50
1996 to 2001	Modified reverse	.50

27

SILVER DOLLARS

1935 Obverse

1936 Obverse

1937 to 1947 Obverse

1935 Reverse

1939 Parliament

1949 Newfoundland

1947
Blunt 7

1947
Pointed 7

1952 Water Lines

1952 No Water Line

1947.

1947 Maple Leaf

GEORGE V 1935 - 1936

Date and Mint Mark	Description	Buying VF Price
1935	Silver Jubilee	13.00
1936	Voyageur	8.00

GEORGE VI 1937 - 1947

Date and Mint Mark	Description	Buying VF Price
1937	Voyageur	8.00
1938	Voyageur	20.00
1939	Royal Visit	3.00
1945	Voyageur	75.00
1946	Voyageur	18.00
1947	Blunt 7	45.00

GEORGE VI 1947 - 1952

Date and Mint Mark	Description	Buy VF P
1947	Pointed 7	60
1947	Maple Leaf	80
1948	Dei Gratia	500
1949	Newfoundland	9
1950	Voyageur	5
1950	Arnprior	5
1951	Voyageur	5
1951	Arnprior	20
1952	Water Lines	5
1952	No Water Lines	5

Arnprior dollars are known to exist in th years 1950, 1951 and 1955. Other year may contain Arnprior varieties but are unknown at the present time.

1953 Obverse

1959 Reverse

1964 Charlottetown

1958 British Columbia

1965 Obverse

1967 Centennial

955 4 Water Lines

1955 2 1/2 Water

1957 4 Water Lines

1957 2 1/2 Water

IZABETH II 1953 to date

te and nt Mark	Description	Buying VF Price
53	Voyageur	3.00
54	Voyageur	5.00
55	Voyageur	5.00
55 Arnprior	One waterline	35.00
56	Voyageur	6.00
57	Voyageur	3.00
57 Arnprior	One Waterline	3.00
58	British Columbia	3.00
59	Voyageur	3.00

ELIZABETH II 1960 - 1967

Date and Mint Mark	Description	Buying VF Price
1960	Voyageur	3.00
1961	Voyageur	3.00
1962	Voyageur	3.00
1963	Voyageur	3.00
1964	Charlottetown	3.00
1965	Voyageur	3.00
1966	Voyageur	3.00
1966 Sm Beads	Voyageur	1,200.00
1967	Centennial	3.00

PORTANT: Do not clean your coins. ins should be handled carefully. Only perts should consider cleaning. If you e not an expert, the results can be astrous.

IMPORTANT: The silver dollar buying prices are for problem free coins in very fine condition. Damaged coins will bring lower prices.

NICKEL DOLLARS

Common Obverse

Voyageur Reverse

Manitoba

British Columbia

Prince Edward Island

Winnipeg

Constitution

Jacques Cartier

ELIZABETH II 1968 - 1974

Date and Mint Mark	Description	Buying Price
1968	Voyageur	1.00
1969	Voyageur	1.00
1970	Manitoba	1.00
1971	British Columbia	1.00
1972	Voyageur	1.00
1973	P.E.I.	1.00
1974	Winnipeg	1.00

ELIZABETH II 1957 - 1987

Date and Mint Mark	Description	Buying Price
1975 to 1981	Voyageur	1.
1982	Constitution	1.
1983	Voyageur	1.
1984	Jacques Cartier	1.
1985	Voyageur	1.
1986	Voyageur	1.
1987	Voyageur	1.

NICKEL BRONZE DOLLARS

ELIZABETH II 1987 - 1989

Date and Mint Mark	Description	Buying Price
1987	Proof	2.00
1987 to 1989	Loon	1.00

ELIZABETH II 1992 - 1993

Date and Mint Mark	Description	Buying Price
1992	Double Date	1.00
1993	Loon	1.00

ELIZABETH II 1990 - 1991

Date and Mint Mark	Description	Buying Price
1990 to 1991	Loon	1.00

ELIZABETH II 1994

Date and Mint Mark	Description	Buying Price
1994	Remembrance Unc	1.00
1994	Remembrance Proof	3.00
1994	Loon	1.00

CANADA 125
Issued to commemorate the 125th birthday of Canada.

ELIZABETH II 1992

Date and Mint Mark	Description	Buying Price
1992	Unc	1.00
1992	Proof	3.00

ELIZABETH II 1995 - 1996

Date and Mint Mark	Description	Buying Price
1995	Peacekeeping Unc	1.00
1995	Peacekeeping Proof	3.00

Note: Proof issues of the 1987, 1992, 1994 and 1995 issue were issued by the Numismatic Department of the Royal Canadian Mint.

ELIZABETH II 1997 - 2001

Date and Mint Mark	Description	Buying Price
1997	For these	
1998	years one dollar	
1999	Loon coins are	
2000	found only in	
2001	RCM Collectors sets	
	See page No. 41	

ELIZABETH II 1995 - 1996

Date and Mint Mark	Description	Buying Price
1995	Loon	1.00
1996	Loon	1.00

TWO DOLLAR COINS

ELIZABETH II 1996 - 1998

Date and Mint Mark	Description	Buying Price
1996	Polar Bear	2.00
1997	Polar Bear	2.00
1998	Polar Bear	2.00
1999	Found only in sets	4.00

ELIZABETH II 2000

Date and Mint Mark	Description	Buying Price
2000	Polar Bears	2.0

ELIZABETH II 1999

Date and Mint Mark	Description	Buying Price
1999	Nunavut	2.00

ELIZABETH II 2000 - 20001

Date and Mint Mark	Description	Buying Price
2000	Polar Bear	2.0
2001	Polar Bear	2.0

GOLD COINS

SOVEREIGNS

WARD VII 1908 - 1910

te and t Mark	Buying Price
)8C	1,100.00
)9C	150.00
0C	135.00

ORGE V 1911 - 1919

te and t Mark	Buying Price
11C	85.00
13C	300.00
14C	150.00
16C	9,000.00
17C	85.00
18C	85.00
19C	85.00

FIVE DOLLARS

ORGE V 1912 - 1914

te and t Mark	Buying Price
12	145.00
13	145.00
14	245.00

TEN DOLLARS

GEORGE V 1912 - 1914

Date and Mint Mark	Buying Price
1912	275.00
1913	275.00
1914	300.00

TWENTY DOLLARS

ELIZABETH II 1967

Date and Mint Mark	Description	Buying Price
1967	Centennial	180.00
1967	Complete Set	190.00

IMPORTANT: Do not clean your coins. Coins should be handled carefully. Only experts should consider cleaning. If you are not an expert, the results can be disastrous.

COLLECTORS ISSUES

The numismatic department of the Royal Canadian Mint issued specially struck a packaged coins starting in 1954. The coins were issued for collectors and as a result are high quality. The dealer buying prices listed below are for single coins and sets in their origin packaging and condition. Coins or sets which have been mishandled or damaged a discounted from the prices listed. Beginning in 1971 the numismatic department of the Roy Canadian Mint issued silver dollars for collectors in two conditions, proof and uncirculate Proof condition dollars were issued in black leatherette boxes while uncirculated dollars we issued in a clear plastic container.

TEN CENTS

Date	Description	Buying Price	Date	Description	Buyi Pri
1997	Caboto silver	7.50	2000	Maison Desjardins silver	7.

TWENTY-FIVE CENTS

Date	Description	No. of Coins	Buyi Pri
1992	125th Anniversary silver proof set	13	50
1992	Single silver coins	1	4
1992	125th Anniversary nickel souvenier set	13	5
1999	Millennium silver proof set	13	50
1999	Single silver coins	1	4
1999	Millennium nickel souvenier set	13	5
2000	Millennium silver proof set	13	50
2000	Single silver coins	1	4
2000	Millennium nickel souvenir set	13	5

FIFTY CENTS
WILD LIFE SERIES

| Atlantic Puffins | Gray Jays | White Tailed Ptarmigans | Whooping Crane |

te	Description	Buying Price	Date	Description	Buying Price
)5	Atlantic Puffins	5.00	1995	White Tailed Ptarmigans	5.00
)5	Gray Jays	5.00	1995	Whooping Crane	5.00

| Black Bear Cubs | Cougar Kittens | Moose Calf | Wood Ducklings |

te	Description	Buying Price	Date	Description	Buying Price
)6	Black Bear Cubs	5.00	1996	Moose Calf	5.00
)6	Cougar Kittens	5.00	1996	Wood Ducklings	5.00

| anadian Eskimo Dog | Labrador Retriever | Newfoundland | Nova Scotia Duck Tolling Retriever |

te	Description	Buying Price	Date	Description	Buying Price
)7	Canadian Eskimo Dog	5.00	1997	Newfoundland	5.00
)7	Labrador Retriever	5.00	1997	Nova Scotia Duck Tolling Retriever	5.00

WILDLIFE SERIES

| Beluga Whale | Blue Whale | Humpback Whale | Killer Whale |

Date	Description	Buying Price	Date	Description	Buying Price
1998	Beluga Whale	5.00	1998	Humpback Whale	5.
1998	Blue Whale	5.00	1998	Killer Whale	5.

| Tonkinese | Lynx | Cymric | Cougar |

Date	Description	Buying Price	Date	Description	Buying Price
1999	Tonkinese	5.00	1999	Cymric	5.
1999	Lynx	5.00	1999	Cougar	5.

SPORTS SERIES

| Auto Racing | Skating | Skiing | Soccer |

Date	Description	Buying Price	Date	Description	Buying Price
1998	Auto Racing	5.00	1998	Skiing	5.0
1998	Skating	5.00	1998	Soccer	5.0

SPORTS SERIES

| Golf | Yacht Race | Basketball | Football |

Date	Description	Buying Price	Date	Description	Buying Price
99	Golf	5.00	1999	Basketball	5.00
99	Yachting	5.00	1999	Football	5.00

| Hockey | Curling | Steeplechase | Bowling |

Date	Description	Buying Price	Date	Description	Buying Price
00	Hockey	5.00	2000	Steeplechase	5.00
00	Curling	5.00	2000	Bowling	5.00

BIRDS OF PREY

| Bald Eagle | Osprey | Great Horned Owl | Red-Tailed Hawk |

Date	Description	Buying Price	Date	Description	Buying Price
00	Bald Eagle	5.00	2000	Great Horned Owl	5.00
00	Osprey	5.00	2000	Red-Tailed Hawk	5.00

SILVER PROOF-LIKE DOLLARS

Issued by the Royal Canadian Mint for collectors. Illustrations of these dollars can be fou
on pages 26 and 27.

Date	Description	Buying Price	Date	Description	Buyi Pri
1954	Voyageur	60.00	1959	Voyageur	5.
1955	Voyageur	50.00	1960	Voyageur	5
1955	Arnprior	75.00	1961	Voyageur	3.
1956	Voyageur	30.00	1962	Voyageur	3.
1957	Voyageur	25.00	1963	Voyageur	3.
1958	British Columbia	20.00	1964	Charlottetown	3.

CASED NICKEL DOLLARS

Manitoba	British Columbia	Prince Edward Island

Winnipeg	Constitution	Jacques Cartier

Date	Description	Buying Price	Date	Description	Buyi Pri
1970	Manitoba	1.00	1975	Voyageur	1.
1971	British Columbia	1.00	1976	Voyageur	1.
1972	Voyageur	1.00	1982	Constitution	2.
1973	Prince Edward Island	1.00	1984	Jacques Cartier	2.
1974	Winnipeg	1.00			

CASED SILVER DOLLARS

Common Obverse

1971 British Columbia

1973 R.C.M.P.

1974 Winnipeg

1975 Calgary

1976 Parliament

1977 Jubilee

1978 Commonwealth

1979 Griffon

Date	Description	Buying Price	Date	Description	Buying Price
1971	British Columbia	2.50	1976	Library of Parliament	2
1972	Voyageur	2.50	1977	Jubilee	2
1973	R.C.M.P.	2.50	1978	Commonwealth Games	2
1974	Winnipeg	2.50	1979	Griffon	4
1975	Calgary Stampede	2.50			

CASED SILVER DOLLARS

1980 Arctic Territories

1981 Trans Canada

1982 Regina

1983 University Games

1984 Toronto

1985 National Parks

1986 Vancouver

1987 Davis Strait

1988 Ironworks

ate	Description	Buying Price	Date	Description	Buying Price
80	Arctic Territories	10.00	1985	National Parks (PF)	4.00
81	Trans Canada (PF)	7.00	1985	National Parks (UNC)	3.00
81	Trans Canada (UNC)	2.50	1986	Vancouver (PF)	4.00
82	Regina (PF)	2.50	1986	Vancouver (UNC)	3.00
82	Regina (UNC)	2.50	1987	Davis Strait (PF)	5.00
83	University Games (PF)	2.50	1987	Davis Strait (UNC)	3.00
83	University Games (UNC)	2.50	1988	Ironworks (PF)	10.00
84	Toronto (PF)	3.00	1988	Ironworks (UNC)	10.00
84	Toronto (UNC)	2.50			

CASED SILVER DOLLARS

1989 MacKenzie River

1990 Henry Kelsey

Common Obverse 1990 to da

1991 Frontenac

1992 Stagecoach

1993 Hockey

1994 R.C.M.P.

1995 325th Anniversary of
Hudson's Bay

1996 McIntosh 200th
Anniversary

Date	Description	Buying Price	Date	Description	Buyi Pri
1989	MacKenzie River (PF)	8.00	1993	Hockey (PF)	7.
1989	MacKenzie River (UNC)	8.00	1993	Hockey (UNC)	4.
1990	Henry Kelsey (PF)	7.00	1994	RCMP (PF)	15.
1990	Henry Kelsey (UNC)	4.00	1994	RCMP (UNC)	10.
1991	Frontenac (PF)	10.00	1995	Hudson's Bay (PF)	10.
1991	Frontenac (UNC)	4.00	1995	Hudson's Bay (UNC)	4.
1992	Stagecoach (PF)	6.00	1996	McIntosh (PF)	10.
1992	Stagecoach (UNC)	4.00	1996	McIntosh (UNC)	5.

CASED SILVER DOLLARS

997 Canada/Russia Hockey

125th Anniversary RCMP

1999 Juan Perez

1999 Older Persons

2000 Voyage of Discovery

Photograph
not
available
at press
time

2001

te	Description	Buying Price	Date	Description	Buying Price
97	Hockey (PF)	10.00	2000	Discovery (PF)	15.00
97	Hockey (UNC)	5.00	2000	Discovery (UNC)	8.00
98	RCMP (PF)	10.00	2001	N/A (PF)	15.00
98	RCMP (UNC)	6.00	2001	N/A (UNC)	8.00
99	Perez (PF)	15.00			
99	Perez (UNC)	8.00			
99	Older Persons (PF)	15.00			
99	Older Persons (UNC)	8.00			

te: **(PR);** Proof condition one dollar coins are issued in a black leatherette case.
(UNC); UNC condition one dollar coins are issued in a clear plastic case.

ONE DOLLAR

Date and Mint Mark	Description	Buying Price
1998	The 1997, 98,	2.0
1998W	99, 2000 and	2.0
1999	2001 Loons are	2.0
2000	found only in	2.0
2000W	RCM sets	2.0

ELIZABETH II 1997 - 2001

Date	Description	Buying Price
1997	Loon	2.00
1997	10th Anniversary	5.00
1997	10th Anniv. Silver	40.00

TWO DOLLARS

ELIZABETH II 1996

Date	Description	Buying Price
1996	Uncirculated	5.00
1996	Proof	10.00
1996	Piedfort	50.00
1996	Gold	200.00

ELIZABETH II 2000

Date	Description	Buying Price
2000	Silver	15.
2000	Gold	150.

ELIZABETH II 1999

Date	Description	Buying Price
1999	Silver	15.00
1999	Gold	150.00

FIVE DOLLAR COIN

ZABETH II 1996

e	Description	Buying Price	Date	Description	Buying Price
6	Bethune	20.00	2000	Viking Settlement	20.00

1976 MONTREAL OLYMPIC COINS

For the Summer Olympic Games of 1976, held in Montreal, seven series of silver coins we minted. There were four different coins in each series. Two $5.00 and two $10.00 coins, stru in sterling silver. The $5.00 coins weigh 24.3 grams and the $10.00 coins weigh 48.6 gram The coins were available, encapsulated in plastic, as single coins, and in custom, prestige a proof four-coin sets. Each set of four coins, with a face value of $30.00, contains 4.28 oz fine silver. The purchase price of these sets is linked to the market price of silver, even if intrinsic value falls below the face value. Large quantities of these coins were issued, and th are not redeemable by the government or the banks.

SERIES I

$5 Map of North America

$5 Kingston

$10 World Map

$10 Montreal

SERIES II

$5 Athlete with Torch

$5 Olive Wreath

$10 Head of Zeus

$10 Temple of Zeus

SERIES III

$5 Canoeing

$5 Rowing

$10 Lacrosse

$10 Bicycling

SERIES IV

$5 The Marathon

$5 Ladies' Javelin

$10 Men's Hurdles

$10 Ladies' Shot Put

SERIES V

$5 The Diver

$5 The Swimmer

$10 The Paddler

$10 Sailing

SERIES VI

$5 Fencing

$5 Boxing

$10 Field Hockey

$10 Football

SERIES VII

$5 Olympic Flame

$5 Olympic Village

$10 Olympic Stadium

$10 Olympic Velodrome

ate	Series	$5 Coin	$10 Coin	Custom Set	Prestige Set	Proof Set
73	1	5.00	10.00	30.00	30.00	30.00
74 Mule		—	100.00	—	—	—
74	2	5.00	10.00	30.00	30.00	30.00
74	3	5.00	10.00	30.00	30.00	30.00
75	4	5.00	10.00	30.00	30.00	30.00
75	5	5.00	10.00	30.00	30.00	30.00
76	6	5.00	10.00	30.00	30.00	32.00
76	7	5.00	10.00	30.00	30.00	35.00

SILVER FIFTEEN DOLLAR COINS

| OLYMPIC CENTENNIAL COINS | LUNAR CALENDER COINS |

Common Obverse

1998 Year of the Tiger

Sports

1999 Year of the Rabbit

Spirit

2000 Year of the Dragon

ELIZABETH II 1992

Date	Description	Buying Price
1992	Sports	20.00
1992	Spirit	70.00

ELIZABETH II 1998-1999

Date	Description	Buying Price
1998	Tiger	35.
1999	Rabbit	35.
2000	Dragon	35.

TWENTY DOLLAR COINS
1988 CALGARY OLYMPIC GAMES

The XV Winter Olympic Games were held in Calgary, February 13th to 29th, 1988. Te[n]
different $20 silver coins were issued to commemorate this event. The coins weigh 34.1[0]
grams, the composition is .925 silver and .075 copper, and they were issued in proof single[s]
or proof sets in one or two coin display cases. Incorporated into the design of these coins a[re]
the letters "XV OLYMPIC WINTER GAMES - XVes JEUX OLYMPIQUE D'HIVER" impresse[d]
into the edge. During the striking of these coins at the Royal Canadian Mint, the impresse[d]
procedures were skipped on some series resulting in the edge lettering being missed on fo[ur]
known coins, resulting in varieties.

FIRST SERIES

Downhill Skiing

Speed Skating

SECOND SERIES

Hockey

Biathalon

THIRD SERIES

Cross-Country Skiing

Free-Style Skiing

FOURTH SERIES

Figure Skating

Curling

FIFTH SERIES

Ski Jumping

Bobsleigh

te	Description	Buying Single	Buying Set
35	Downhill Skiing	20.00	
35	Speed Skating	20.00	40.00
35	Speed Skating, no edge lettering	100.00	
36	Hockey	20.00	
36	Hockey, no edge lettering	100.00	
36	Biathalon	20.00	40.00
36	Biathalon, no edge lettering	100.00	
36	Cross-Country Skiing	20.00	
36	Free-Style Skiing	20.00	40.00
36	Free-Style Skiing, no edge lettering	100.00	
37	Figure Skating	20.00	
37	Curling	20.00	40.00
37	Ski Jumping	20.00	
37	Bobsleigh	20.00	40.00

TWENTY DOLLAR COINS

AVIATION
FIRST SERIES 1990 - 1994

Canada's aviation heroes and their achievements are commemorated on this first series twenty dollar sterling-silver coins. The series is made up of ten coins, which were issued t per year over five years. For the first time, each coin design contains a 24-karat-gold -cover oval cameo portrait of the aviation hero commemorated. A maximum of 50,000 of each c was offered for sale.

Coin No. 1
Anson and Harvard/Leckie

Coin No. 2
Lancaster/Fauquier

Coin No. 3 A.E.A. Silver Dart
F.W. Baldwin, John A. D.

Coin No. 4 de Havilland
Beaver/

Coin No. 5 Curtiss UN-4/
Sir F.W. Ballie

Coin No. 6 de Havilland
Gypsy Moth/ Murton A.

Coin No.7
Fairchild 71C/J.A.Richardson

Coin No. 8
Super Electra/Z.L.Leigh

Coin No. 9
Curtiss HS-2L/Stuart Graham

Coin No. 10
Vickers Vedette/T. Reid

ate	Coin No.	Description	Buying Price
90	1	Anson and Harvard/Leckie	35.00
90	2	Lancaster/Fauquier	100.00
91	3	Silver Dart/Baldwin, McCurdy	30.00
91	4	Beaver/Garratt	30.00
92	5	Curtiss/Baille	30.00
92	6	Gypsy Moth/Seymour	30.00
93	7	Fairchild/Richardson	30.00
93	8	Super Electra/Leigh	30.00
94	9	Curtiss/Graham	30.00
94	10	Vedette/Reid	30.00

AVIATION
SECOND SERIES 1995 - 1999

This second series of aviation coins celebrates "Powered Flight in Canada — Beyond Wo War II. As with the first series, it is made up of ten coins to be issued two per year over fi years. Each coin design contains a 24-karat-gold-covered oval cameo portrait of the pil engineers or designers of the aircrafts. A maximum of 50,000 of each coin is offered for sa

Coin No.11
The Fleet 80 Canuck/ Noury

Coin No. 12
DHC-1 Chipmunk/ Bannock

Coin No. 13
CF-100 Canuck/Zurakowski

Coin No. 14
CF-105 Arrow/Chamberlin

Date	Coin No.	Description	Buyi Pri
1995	11	Fleet 80 Canuck/Noury	35
1995	12	DHC-1 Chipmunk/Bannock	35
1996	13	CF-100 Canuck/Zurakowski	35
1996	14	CF-105 Arrow/Chamberlin	35

Coin No.15
F-86/Villeneuve

Coin No. 16
CT-11T/Tutor

Coin No. 17
CP-107 Argus/Longhurst

Coin No. 18
CL-218/Gagnon

Coin No. 19
Twin Otter/Neal

Coin No. 20
Dash 8/Fowler

ate	Coin No.	Description	Buying Price
97	15	F-86/Villeneuve	35.00
97	16	CT-11T/Tutor	35.00
98	17	CP-107 Argus/Longhurst	35.00
98	18	CL-215 Waterbomber/Gagnon	35.00
99	19	Twin Otter/Neal	35.00
99	20	Dash 8/Fowler	35.00

TRANSPORTATION COMMEMORATIVES
TWENTY DOLLARS

Canada's first sterling silver hologram cameo twenty dollar ocins were issued in 2000. Th new series will commemorate the Canadian Achievement in Transportation. Each coin bea a 24 karat goldplated holographic cameo.

2000 Obverse

Coin # 1
The Bluenose
J. Franklin Wright
Stanley Witten

Coin # 2
The Toronto
John Mardon
Stanley Witten/Cosme Saffioti

Coin # 3
H. S. Taylor Steam Buggy
John Mardon
Cosme Saffioti

Date	Coin No.	Description	Buyi Pr
2000	1	Bluenose	30.
2000	2	Toronto	30
2000	3	Steam Buggy	30
2000		3 coin set	20.

GOLD COINS

ONE HUNDRED DOLLARS

Canada issued the first one-hundred-dollar gold coin in 1976 to commemorate the Montreal Olympic Games. In that year two qualities and proportions of fineness were released; uncirculated coins were .585 fine (14 karat), and proof coins were .925 fine (22 karat). From 1976 to 1986, only proof quality coins with a fineness of .925 were issued. In 1987 the quality remained the same (proof), but the fineness of the coin was altered to .585 fine, or 14 karat, again.

IMPORTANT

Proof coins must be in mint-state condition. Mishandled, mounted or damaged coins are discounted from the prices listed. The buying price for gold coins is tied to the market price of gold. Any movement in the gold price will result in a corresponding price movement for these coins.

1976 - 14 kt   1976 - 22 kt

1977   1978   1979   1980

1981   1982   1983   1984

Date	Description	Fineness	Buying Price	Date	Description	Fineness	Buying Price
76	14 kt Olympic	.585	105.00	1980	Arctic Territories	.916	180.00
76	22 kt Olympic	.916	180.00	1981	"O Canada"	.916	180.00
77	Jubilee	.916	180.00	1982	Constitution	.916	180.00
78	Unity	.916	180.00	1983	Gilbert's Landing	.916	180.00
79	Year of the Child	.916	180.00	1984	Voyage of Discovery	.916	180.00

ONE HUNDRED DOLLARS

1985	1986	1987	1988
1989	1990	1991	1992
1993	1994	1995	1996
1997	1998	1999	2000

Date	Description	Fineness	Buying Price	Date	Description	Fineness	Buying Price
1985	National Parks	.916	180.00	1994	The Home Front	.585	120.
1986	Peace	.916	180.00	1995	Louisbourg	.585	120.
1987	Winter Olympic Games	.585	105.00	1996	Klondike Gold Rush	.585	140.
1988	Bowhead Whale	.585	105.00	1997	Alexander Graham Bell	.585	150.
1989	Ste. Marie	.585	105.00	1998	Insulin	.585	175.
1990	Literacy Year	.585	105.00	1999	Newfoundland	.585	175.
1991	Empress of India	.585	105.00	2000	Northwest Passage	.585	175.
1992	Montreal	.585	110.00	2001	N/A	.585	175.
1993	Horseless Carriage	.585	110.00				

TWO HUNDRED DOLLARS

1990   1991   1992   1993

1994   1995   1996   1997

1998   1999   2000

Photograph
not
available
at press
time

2001

Date	Description	Fineness	Buying Price	Date	Description	Fineness	Buying Price
90	Canada Flag	.916	200.00	1996	Transcontinental	.916	250.00
91	A National Passion	.916	200.00	1997	Haida	.916	275.00
92	Niagara Falls	.916	210.00	1998	White Buffalo	.916	275.00
93	RCMP	.916	210.00	1999	Butterfly	.916	275.00
94	Anne of Green Gables	.916	210.00	2000	Mother and Child	.916	275.00
95	Sugar Bush	.916	225.00	2001	N/A	—	—

175 AND 350 DOLLAR GOLD COINS

175 DOLLAR GOLD COIN

350 DOLLAR GOLD COINS

2000
Photograph
not
available
at press
time

ELIZABETH II 1992

Date	Description	Buying Price
1992	Olympic	200.00

ELIZABETH II 1998-1999

Date	Description	Buying Price
1998	90th Anniversary	450.0
1999	Golden Slipper	450.0
2000	Pacific Dogwood	450.0

PROOF PLATINUM COINS

In 1990 the Royal Canadian Mint entered the luxury market for high-quality collector coin
The platinum coin sets are comprised of four coins all depicting some facet of the life of th
animal in its natural habitat. The coin denominations in the sets are $300, $150, $75 and $3

1990 Polar Bears   1991 Snowy Owls   1992 Cougars

1993 Arctic Foxes   1994 Otters   1995 Lynx

1996 Peregrine Falcons   1997 Wood Bisons   1998 Wolves

Date	Description	Buying Price	Date	Description	Buyin Pric
1990	Polar Bear Set	1,000.00	1997	Bison Set	1,500.0
1991	Snowy Owl Set	1,000.00	1997	Bison $30	65.0
1992	Cougar Set	1,100.00	1997	Bison $150	325.0
1993	Arctic Fox Set	1,100.00	1998	Wolf Set	1,500.0
1994	Otter Set	1,100.00	1998	Wolf $30	65.0
1995	Lynx Set	1,250.00	1998	Wolf $150	325.0
1995	Lynx $30	65.00	1999	Muskox Set	1,500.0
1995	Lynx $150	325.00	1999	Muskox $30	65.0
1996	Falcon Set	1,250.00	2000	Pronghorn Set	1,500.0
1996	Falcon $30	65.00	2000	Pronghorn $30	65.0
1996	Falcon $50	325.00			

MAPLE LEAF BULLION COINS

he Maple Leaf gold coins were first produced in 1979, the fractional or small sizes three
ars later in 1982, and the half-ounce size in 1986. In 1988 the four sizes; $5.00, $10.00,
0.00 and $50.00, of platinum were added. Expanding the range in 1993, $1.00 gold and
atinum coins were issued, and again in 1994 $2.00 coins were placed on the market.
he price of Maple Leaf bullion coins is based on the spot market on the day of purchase,
nes their gold content, less a small handling charge.

$50 $20 $10 $5

COIN SPECIFICATIONS

nomination	Description	Content	Weight Tr. Oz.
	1/20 Maple	Gold or platinum	.050
	1/15 Maple	Gold or platinum	.667
	1/10 Maple	Gold or platinum	.100
)	1/4 Maple	Gold or platinum	.250
)	1/2 Maple	Gold or platinum	.500
0	Maple	Gold or platinum	1.00
	Maple	Silver	1.00
)	10 Maple	Silver	10.00

MAPLE LEAF PROOF BULLION ISSUES OF 1989

o commemorate the tenth anniversary of the Maple Leaf bullion program, the Royal
anadian Mint, in 1989, issued a series of proof condition silver, gold and platinum coins,
dividually and in sets. The single coins and sets were packaged in solid maple presentation
ses with brown velvet liners.

pe	Description	Buying Price
ts	Gold 4 coins: 1, 1/2, 1/4, 1/10 ounce maple	800.00
	Platinum 4 coins: 1, 1/2, 1/4, 1/4, 1/10 ounce maple	1,000.00
	Gold and Platinum 1/10 ounce maple each, Silver 1 ounce Maple, 3 coins	115.00
	Gold, Platinum and Silver 3 coins: 1 ounce maple each	1,100.00
gles	Gold, One Maple	450.00
	Silver, One Maple	20.00

COLLECTOR SETS

SILVER PROOF-LIKE SETS

Date	Description	Buying Price
1954	Voyageur	160.00
1955	Voyageur	110.00
1955	Arnprior	135.00
1956	Voyageur	65.00
1957	Voyageur	35.00
1958	British Columbia	30.00
1959	Voyageur	15.00
1960	Voyageur	78.00
1961	Voyageur	78.00
1962	Voyageur	7.00
1963	Voyageur	7.00
1964	Charlottetown	7.00
1965	Voyageur	7.00
1966	Voyageur	7.00
1967	Centennial	8.00

NICKEL PROOF-LIKE 6 COIN SETS

Date	Description	Buying Price
1968	Voyageur	2.00
1969	Voyageur	2.00
1970	Manitoba	2.00
1971	British Columbia	2.00
1972	Voyageur	2.00
1973	R.C.M.P., Small Bust	2.00
1973	R.C.M.P., Large Bust	75.00
1974	Winnipeg	2.00
1975	Voyageur	2.00
1976	Voyageur	2.00
1977	Voyageur	2.00
1978	Voyageur	2.00
1979	Voyageur	2.00
1980	Voyageur	3.00
1981	Voyageur	2.00
1982	Voyageur	2.00
1983	Voyageur	3.00
1984	Voyageur	3.00
1985	Voyageur	3.00
1986	Voyageur	4.00
1987	Voyageur	3.00
1988	Loon	3.00
1989	Loon	5.00
1990	Loon	5.00
1991	Loon	15.00
1992	Loon	8.00
1993	Loon	4.00
1994	Loon	4.00
1994	"O Canada"	5.00

NICKEL PROOF-LIKE 6 COIN SETS

Date	Description	Buying Pric
1995	Loon	4.0
1995	"O Canada"	5.0
1995	"Tiny Treasures"	6.0
1996	Loon/Polar Bear	10.0
1996	"O Canada"	9.0
1996	"Tiny Treasures"	9.0

NICKEL PROOF-LIKE 7 COIN SETS

Date	Description	Buying Pric
1997	Loon/Polar Bear	6.0
1997	"O Canada"	8.0
1997	"Tiny Treasures"	8.0
1998W	Loon/Polar Bear	15.0
1998	Loon/Polar Bear	8.0
1998W	"O Canada"	10.0
1998W	"Tiny Treasures"	10.0
1999	Loon/Polar Bear	8.0
1999	Loon/Nunavut	8.0
1999	"O Canada"	8.0
1999	"Tiny Treasures"	8.0
2000	Loon/Polar Bear	8.0
2000W	Loon/Polar Bear	8.0
2000	Loon/Polar Bears	8.0
2000	"O Canada"	10.0
2000W	"O Canada"	10.0
2000	"Tiny Treasures"	10.0
2000W	"Tiny Treasures"	10.0

CUSTOM 7 COIN SETS

Date	Description	Buying Pric
1971 to 1980		2.0

SPECIMEN 6 COIN SETS

Date	Description	Buying Pric
1981	Voyageur	3.0
1982	Voyageur	3.0
1983	Voyageur	3.5
1984	Voyageur	3.5
1985	Voyageur	3.5
1986	Voyageur	3.5
1987	Voyageur	3.5
1988	Loon	4.0
1989	Loon	6.0
1990	Loon	6.0
1991	Loon	15.0
1992	Loon	9.0
1993	Loon	6.0
1994	Loon	8.0
1995	Loon	8.0
1996	Loon	10.0

ECIMEN 7 COIN SETS

te	Description	Buying Price
7	Flying loon	10.00
8	Loon/Polar Bear	10.00
9	Loon/Polar Bear	10.00
0	Loon/Polar Bear	10.00
0	Loon/Polar Bears	10.00
1	Loon/Polar Bear	10.00

ESTIGE 7 COIN SETS

te	Description	Buying Price
1	British Columbia	8.00
2	Voyageur	10.00
3	R.C.M.P., Small Bust	8.00
3	R.C.M.P., Large Bust	75.00
4	Winnipeg	8.00
5	Calgary	8.00
6	Parliament	8.00
7	Jubilee	8.00
8	Commonwealth Games	8.00
9	Griffon	10.00
0	Arctic Territories	18.00
1	Trans Canada	14.00
2	Regina	9.00
3	University Games	9.00
4	Toronto	9.00
5	National Parks	9.00
6	Vancouver	9.00
7	Davis Straits	10.00
8	Ironworks	18.00
9	MacKenzie River	18.00
0	Henry Kelsey	18.00
1	Frontenac	35.00
2	Stagecoach	25.00
3	Hockey	15.00
4	RCMP	20.00
4	RCMP Red Box	20.00
5	Hudson's Bay	30.00
5	Hudson's Bay Red Box	25.00
6	John McIntosh	35.00

ESTIGE 8 COIN SETS

e	Description	Buying Price
7	Canada/Russia Hockey	40.00
8	RCMP 125th Anniversary	40.00
9	Juan Perez	40.00
0	N/A	40.00

PROOF SETS

Sets of specimen coins have been issued in Canada at various times since 1858, often in official cases. A representative selection follows. Sets from 1908 are in leather or leatherette-covered presentation cases

Date	Description	Buying Price
1858	Victoria:	
	1, 5, 10, 20 cents	3,000.00
1870	Victoria:	
	5, 10, 25, 50 cents	8,000.00
1908	Edward VII:	
	1, 5, 10, 25, 50 cents	1,000.00
1911	George V:	
	1, 5, 10, 25, 50 cents	3,000.00
1937	George VI:	
	1, 5, 10, 25, 50 cents $1	500.00
1937	George VI:	
	as above, but in card case	250.00
1967	Elizabeth II: Centennial,	
	1, 5, 10, 25, 50 cents	
	$1.00, $20.00 gold	175.00
1967	Elizabeth II: Centennial,	
	as above, but with medal	
	instead of $20.00 gold	10.00
1998	Elizabeth II: Reissued 1908-1998	
	Matte	50.00
	Proof	50.00

PAPER MONEY OF CANADA

PROVINCE OF CANADA

1866 ISSUES

Denom.	Issue Date	Buying Price	Denom.	Issue Date	Buying Price
$1	1866	500.00	$10	1866	2,500.0
$2	1866	1,200.00	$20	1866	3,500.0
$5	1866	1,800.00	$50	1866	6,000.0

CANADA

1870 ISSUES

Plain

Series Letter A

Series Letter B

Denom.	Issue Date	Buying Price	Denom.	Issue Date	Buying Price
25-cent Plain	1870	12.00	25-cent Series B	1870	15.
25-cent Series A	1870	75.00			

Note: Buying prices are for notes in VG condition

68

1870 ISSUES

nom.	Issue Date	Variety/Signature	Buying Price
	1870	Payable at Montreal or Toronto	275.00
	1870	Payable at Halifax	450.00
	1870	Payable at St. John	450.00
	1870	Payable at Montreal or Toronto	1,500.00
	1870	Payable at Halifax or St. John	2,500.00

1878 ISSUES

nom.	Issue Date	Variety/Signature	Buying Price
	1878	Scalloped Frame, Payable at Montreal or Toronto	250.00
	1878	Scalloped Frame, Payable at St. John or Halifax	750.00
	1878	Lettered Frame, Payable at Montreal or Toronto	75.00
	1878	Lettered Frame, Payable at St. John or Halifax	450.00
	1878	Payable at Montreal or Toronto	750.00
	1878	Payable at St. John or Halifax	1,500.00

1882 AND 1887 ISSUES

nom.	Issue Date	Variety/Signature	Buying Price
	1882		750.00
	1887	Plain, Series A	300.00

1897 AND 1898 ISSUES

No "One"	Inward "One"	Outward "One"

Denom.	Issue Date	Variety/Signature	Buyi Pri
$1	1897	Green face tint	200.
$2	1897	Red-brown back	450.
$2	1897	Dark brown back	100.
$1	1898	Inward "One"	60.
$1	1898	Outward "One"	40.

1900 AND 1902 ISSUES

"4" on Top	"Four" on Top

Denom.	Issue Date	Variety/Signature	Buyi Pri
25-cent	1900	Courtney	2.
25-cent	1900	Bouville	2.
25-cent	1900	Saunders	2.
$4	1900		375.
$4	1902	"4" on Top	400.
$4	1902	"Four" on Top	375.

Note: All buying prices are for notes in very good condition.

1911 AND 1912 ISSUES

| No Seal | Seal over Five | Seal Only |

nom.	Issue Date	Variety/Signature	Buying Price
	1911	Green Line or Black Line	30.00
0	1911		5,000.00
000	1911		5,000.00
	1912	No Seal	200.00
	1912	Seal over Five	250.00
	1912	Seal Only	200.00

1914 AND 1917 ISSUES

nom.	Issue Date	Variety/Signature	Buying Price
	1914	No Seal	50.00
	1914	Seal over Two	125.00
	1914	Seal Only	75.00
	1917	No Seal	25.00
	1917	Seal over One	30.00
	1917	Black Seal	25.00

1923 ISSUES

Denom.	Issue Date	Variety/Signature	Buying Price
25-cent	1923	Hyndman/Saunders	2.
25-cent	1923	McCavour/Saunders	2.
25-cent	1923	Campbell/Clark	2
$1	1923	Various Colour Seals	20.
$1	1923	Purple Seal	40.
$2	1923	Various Colours Seals	30
$2	1923	Green Seal	28.
$2	1923	Bronze Seal	28.

1924 AND 1925 ISSUES

Denom.	Issue Date	Variety/Signature	Buying Price
$5	1924	Queen Mary	1,000
$500	1925	George V	6,000
$1,000	1925	Queen Mary	6,500.

Note: All buying prices are for notes in very good condition.

1935 ISSUES

om.	Variety	Buying Price
	English text	10.00
	French text	15.00
	English text	15.00
	French text	30.00
	English text	30.00
	French text	40.00
	English text	30.00
	French text	40.00
	English text, small seal	75.00
	English text, large seal	100.00

Denom.	Variety	Buying Price
$20	French text	175.00
$25	English text	500.00
$25	French text	600.00
$50	English text	250.00
$50	French text	300.00
$100	English text	150.00
$100	French text	250.00
$500	English or French	7,500.00
$1,000	English or French	1,100.00

1937 ISSUES

IMPORTANT

Bank notes with tears, missing corners, pinholes or folding creases are not considered to very fine (VF). Notes in poor condition are not collectable.

Denom.	Very Fine Buying Prices By Signature		
	Osborne	Gordon	Coyn
$1	5.00	3.00	3.0
$2	7.00	5.00	5.0
$5	20.00	6.00	6.0
$10	14.00	10.00	10.0
$20	25.00	20.00	20.0
$50	100.00	50.00	50.0
$100	110.00	100.00	100.0
$1,000	1,025.00	Not Issued	

1954 ISSUES

"DEVIL'S FACE" PORTRAIT

IMPORTANT

ne buying prices listed below are for notes in extremely fine condition. The notes must be
an with no tears, pinholes or noticeable folds or creases.

THE DEVIL'S FACE NOTES

On the earliest notes of the 1954 issue,
highlighted areas of the Queen's hair
produced the illusion of a leering demonic
face behind her ear. This was not the result of
an error, nor was it, as some have asserted,
the prank of an IRA sympathizer at the bank
note company. It was merely the faithful
reproduction of the original photograph. The
portrait of the Queen with the devil's face
outlined in her hair generated almost instant
controversy.

ASTERISK NOTES

Asterisk notes are replacement notes, the
first being spoiled in printing, cutting, etc., and
replaced by an asterisk note.

om.	Very Fine Buying Price by Signature			
	Coyne/Towers		Beattie/Coyne	
	Regular	Asterisk	Regular	Asterisk
	3.00	150.00	2.00	100.00
	3.50	200.00	3.00	150.00
	7.00	400.00	7.00	200.00
	11.00	300.00	11.00	200.00
	22.00	350.00	20.00	250.00
	50.00	NI	50.00	NI
	100.00	NI	100.00	NI
)0	1,000.00	NI	NI	NI

- Not Issued

MODIFIED PORTRAIT

IMPORTANT

The buying prices listed below are for notes in uncirculated condition (new). The note mu be clean, crisp, with no tears, creases, folds or marks of any kind or description.

MODIFIED PORTRAIT

The portrait was modified by darkening highlights in the hair and thus removing shading which had resulted in the devil's fa The modification of the face plates was ma for most denominations in 1956, except the $1,000 denomination, which was modif several years later.

	Uncirculated Buying Price by Signature							
	Beattie/Coyne		Beattie/Rasminsky		Bouey/Raminsky		Lawson/Bou	
Denom.	Regular	Astrisk	Regular	Asterisk	Regular	Asterisk	Regular	Aster
$1	1.75	10.00	1.75	3.00	1.75	3.00	1.75	2.0
$2	6.00	20.00	2.50	4.00	2.50	3.00	2.50	4.0
$5	10.00	20.00	7.50	10.00	10.00	15.00	NI	N
$10	15.00	25.00	12.50	15.00	NI	NI	NI	N
$20	30.00	40.00	25.00	40.00	NI	NI	NI	N
$50	60.00	NI	55.00	NI	NI	NI	100.00	N
$100	105.00	NI	105.00	NI	NI	NI	105.00	N
$1,000	1,000.00	NI	1,000.00	NI	1,000.00	NI	1,000.00	N

*NI - Not Issued

$1 CENTENNIAL 1967

or the centennial of Canada's Confederation a special $1 note was issued. The note has a
gle design and two types of serial numbers, regular serial numbers and a special number
367 - 1967." The special series was available from the Bank of Canada as a collector's item,
t examples were soon found in circulation. In addition, there was an asterisk note series for
placement notes.

nom.	Issue Date	Variety	Uncirculated Buying Price
	1967	Commemorative Serial Number 1867-1967	1.25
	1967	Regular Serial Number	1.25
	1967	Asterisk Serial Number	2.00

1969 - 1975 ISSUE

his new series combined fine line engraving with subtle variations to make notes that are
remely difficult to counterfeit. The series features a new portrait of the Queen, as well as
traits of previous prime ministers of Canada.

IMPORTANT

he buying prices listed on the following page are for notes in uncirculated condition (new).
e note must be clean, crisp, with no tears, creases, folds or marks of any kind or description.

ASTERISK AND "X" REPLACEMENT NOTES

Replacement of defective notes by asterisk notes was continued when the 1968-1975 iss
was introduced. The highest denomination of the 1954 issue to be printed with asterisks w
the $20; however, all denominations in the 1969-1975 issue, including the $50 and $100 note
occur with asterisks in front of the two-letter prefix type.

When the triple-letter prefix notes were introduced in 1981, the use of the asterisk w
discontinued. For triple-letter prefix notes, a replacement note was then designated by the u
of an "X" for the third letter.

Asterisk Notes
BC-46aA

"X" Replacement Notes
BC-46A-i

	Uncirculated Buying Price by Signature							
	Beattie/Rasminsky		Bouey/Rasminsky		Lawson/Bouey		Crow/Bouey	
Denom.	Regular	Asterisk	Regular	Asterisk	Regular	Asterisk	Regular	Asteri
$1	NI	NI	NI	NI	1.25	1.50	1.00	1.5(
$2	NI	NI	NI	NI	2.25	4.00	2.00	20.0(
$5	NI	NI	7.50	10.00	7.00	8.00	NI	N
$10	15.00	20.00	20.00	15.00	12.00	15.00	12.00	15.0(
$20	22.00	25.00	NI	NI	22.00	25.00	NI	N
$50	NI	NI	NI	NI	50.00	60.00	50.00	55.0
$100	NI	NI	NI	NI	100.00	105.00	100.00	105.0(

Note: The Thiessen/Crow combination of signatures does not command a numismatic premium
at this time.

*NI - Not Issued

1979 ISSUES

The series beginning in 1979 is a modification of the previous issue. The face designs are similar, as is the colouration. The serial numbers are moved to the back of the note at the bottom, where the name of the Bank of Canada previously appeared. The black serial numbers are machine readable.

IMPORTANT

The buying prices listed below are for notes in uncirculated condition (new). The note must be clean, crisp, with no tears, creases, folds or marks of any kind or description.

REPLACEMENT NOTES

There are no asterisk notes in this issue. The replacement notes are designated by the second digit in the serial number.

The digit 1 following the first digit 3 of the $5 notes designates a replacement note. In the 20 denomination the replacement notes can be distinguished by "510" for the CBN company and "516" for the BABN company.

| $5 Replacement Note | $20 Replacement Note |

nom.	Uncirculated Buying Price by Signature					
	Lawson/Bouey		Crow/Bouey		Thiessen/Crow	
	Regular	Asterisk	Regular	Astrisk	Reguar	Asterisk
	7.50	30.00	7.50	60.00	NI	NI
	25.00	30.00	20.00	25.00	20.00	25.00

1986 ISSUES

On March 14, 1986, the Bank of Canada introduced a new series of bank notes. The ne[w] designs were launched that year with the issue of the $2 and $5 notes. The $1 and $2 ba[nk] notes have been replaced with $1 and $2 coins.

$5 Replacement Note

	Uncirculated Buying Price by Signature					
	Crow/Bouey		Thiessen/Crow		Bonin/Thiessen	
Denom.	Regular	Asterick	Regular	Asterick	Regular	Asterick
$2	4.00	8.00	3.00	5.00	2.00	10.00
$5	8.00	20.00	5.00	8.00	5.00	15.00
$10	N/I	N/I	11.00	15.00	10.00	15.00
$20	N/I	N/I	21.00	25.00	20.00	25.00
$50	N/I	N/I	55.00	60.00	50.00	N/I
$100	N/I	N/I	100.00	110.00	100.00	N/I
$1000	N/I	N/I	1,000.00	1,200.00	1,000.00	N/I

NEWFOUNDLAND PUBLIC WORKS CASH NOTES

PRINCE EDWARD ISLAND

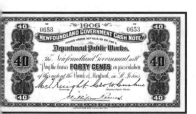

1901-1909

nom.	Buying Price
cents	75.00
cents	85.00
cents	100.00
	125.00
	500.00

Denom.	Buying Price
1848-1870 £1	300.00
1872 $10	250.00
1872 $20	250.00

NOVA SCOTIA

1910-1911

nom.	Buying Price
cents	35.00
cents	35.00
	50.00
	450.00
	600.00

Denom.	Buying Price
1848-1854 £1	100.00
1861 $5	200.00

GOVERNMENT NOTES

nom.	Buying Price
	40.00
	75.00

CANADIAN NOTE-ISSUING BANKS

The following list of banks identifies in alphabetical order all the non-government banks whic issued or ordered Canadian notes.

Bank notes were first issued in Canada in 1813 and continued until 1943. One hundred an sixty different banks issued notes and some over a long period of time. There are litera thousands of different notes and if you add different grades, the number rises to tens thousands. Far beyond the scope of this guide.

If you have a bank note that is on this list of banks then it is Canadian and please check wi your local dealer for current buying prices.

The Bank of Acadia, Liverpool, N.S., 1872-1873
The Accommodation Bank, Kingston, U.C., 1836-1837
The Agricultural Bank, Montreal, L.C., 1837
The Agricultural Bank, Toronto, U.C., 1834-1837
Arman's Bank, Montreal, L.C., 1837
Barclay's Bank (Canada), Montreal, Que., 1929-1956
La Banque du Boucherville, Boucherville, L.C., 1830's
The Bank of Brantford, Brantford, C.W., 1857-1860's
The British Canadian Bank, Toronto, Ont., 1883-1884
The Bank of British Columbia, Victoria, B.C., 1862-1901
The Bank of British North America, 1836-1918
Canada Bank, Montreal, L.C., 1792
The Canada Bank, Toronto, C.W., 1855
The Bank of Canada, Montreal, L.C., 1813-1831
The Canadian Bank of Commerce, Toronto, Ont., 1867-1961
Banque Canadienne, St. Hyacinthe, L.C., 1836-1838
Banque Canadienne Nationale, Montreal, Que., 1924-1979
The Central Bank of Canada, Toronto, Ont., 1883-1887
Central Bank of New Brunswick, Fredericton, N.B., 1834-1866
Charlotte County Bank, St. Andrew's, N.B., 1825-1865
Bank of Charlottetown, Charlottetown, P.E.I., 1852
The City Bank, Montreal, L.C., 1833-1876
City Bank, Saint John, N.B., 1836-1839
The Bank of Clifton, C.W., 1859-1863
The Colonial Bank of Canada, Toronto, C.W., 1856-1863
The Colonial Bank of Chatham, Chatham, U.C., 1837-1839
Commerical Bank, Brockville, U.C., 1837
Commercial Bank, Kingston, U.C., 1837
The Commercial Bank of Canada, Kingston, C.W., 1856-1868
The Commercial Bank of Fort Erie, Fort Erie, U.C., 1836-1839
The Commercial Bank of Lake Ontario, Niagara Falls, U.C., 1837
The Commercial Bank of Manitoba, Winnipeg, Man., 1885-1893
The Commerical Bank of the Midland District, Kingston, U.C., 1831-1856
Commerical Bank of Montreal, Montreal, L.C., 1835-1837
Commercial Bank of New Brunswick, Saint John, N.B., 1834-1868
The Commercial Bank of Newfoundland, St. John's, Nfld., 1857-1894
Commercial Bank of Windsor, Windsor, N.S., 1864-1902
Commerical Branch Bank of Canada, Collingwood, C.W., 1861-1879
The Consolidated Bank of Canada, Montreal, Que., 1876-1879
The Bank of the County of Elgin, St. Thomas, C.W., 1857-1862
The Crown Bank of Canada, Toronto, Ont., 1904-1908
The Dominion Bank, Toronto, Ont., 1869-1955
Eastern Bank of Canada, Saint John, N.B., 1928-1934
The Eastern Townships Bank, Sherbrooke, C.E., 1855-1912
The Exchange Bank, Quebec, L.C., 1840's
The Exchange Bank of Canada, Montreal, Que., 1871-1883
The Exchange Bank of Canada, Windsor, Ont., 1860's

The Exchange Bank of Toronto, C.W., 1855
The Exchange Bank of Yarmouth, Yarmouth, N.S., 1867-1903
The Exchange Bank Company of Chippewa, Chippewa, U.C., 1837
The Farmer's Bank, Toronto, U.C., 1840's
The Farmers Bank of Canada, Toronto, Ont., 1906-1910
The Farmer's Bank of Malden, Maiden, U.C., 1840's
The Farmer's Joint Stock Banking Co., Toronto, U.C., 1835-1849
The Farmers J.S. Banking Co., Toronto, U.C., 1830's
The Farmers Bank of Rustico, Rustico, P.E.I., 1862-1892
The Farmers Bank of St. John's, St. John's, L.C., 1837-1838
The Federal Bank of Canada, Toronto, Ont., 1874-1888
The Bank of Fredericton, Fredericton, N.B., 1836-1839
The Free Holders Bank of the Midland District, Bath, U.C., 1837
Goderich Bank, Goderich, U.C., 1834
The Gore Bank, Hamilton, U.C., 1835-1870
The Gore Bank of Hamilton, Hamilton, U.C., c.1837
The Grenville County Bank, Prescott, C.W., 1856
The Halifax Banking Company, Halifax, N.S., 1825-1903
The Hamtilon Bank, Hamilton, L.C., 1835
The Bank of Hamilton, Hamilton, Ont., 1872-1923
Hart's Bank, Three Rivers, L.C., 1835-1847
Henry's Bank, La Prairie and Montreal, L.C., 1837
Banque d'Hochelaga, Montreal, Que., 1873-1925
The Home Bank of Canada, Toronto, Ont., 1903-1923
The Bank of Hull, Hull, L.C., 1837
The Imperial Bank of Canada, Toronto, Ont., 1873-1961
The International Bank of Canada, Toronto, U.C., 1858-1859
Banque Internationale du Canada, Montreal, Que., 1911-1913
La Banque Jacques Cartier, Montreal, C.E., 1861-1900
The Kingston Bank, Kingston, L.C., 1837
The Bank of Liverpool, Liverpool, N.S., 1871-1879
The Bank of London in Canada, London, Ont., 1883-1888
Lower Canada Bank, Montreal, L.C., 1837
The Bank of Lower Canada, Quebec, L.C., late 1830's MacDonald & Co., Victoria, B.C.,
    1859-1866
The Maritime Bank of the Dominon of Canada, Saint John, N.B., 1872-1887
The Mechanics Bank, Montreal, L.C., 1837
The Mechanics Bank, Montreal, C.E., 1865-1879
The Mechanics Bank of Saint John's, Saint John's, L.C., 1837
The Mercantile Banking Corporation, Halifax, N.S., 1878
The Merchants Bank, Montreal, C.E., 1864-1868
The Merchants Bank, Toronto, U.C., 1837
The Merchants Bank of Canada, Montreal, Que., 1868-1923
The Merchants Bank of Halifax, Halifax, N.S., 1864-1901
The Merchants Bank of Prince Edward Island, Charlottetown, P.E.I., 1871-1906
The Merchants Exchange Bank, Goderich, C.W., 1853
The Metropolitan Bank, Montreal, Que., 1871-1876
The Metropolitan Bank, Toronto, 1902-1914
The Molsons Bank, Montreal, C.E., 1837-1925
Montreal Bank, Montreal, L.C., 1817-1822
The Montreal Bank, Montreal, C.W., 1840's-1950's
The Bank of Montreal, Montreal, L.C., 1822 to date
La Banque Nationale, Montreal, C.E., 1860-1925
The Bank of New Brunswick, Saint John, N.B., 1820-1913
The Newcastle Banking Co., Amherst, U.C., 1836
The Newcastle District Loan Company, Peterborough, U.C., 1836
The Newcastle District Bank, St. Catharines, C.W., 1853-1875
The Niagara Suspension Bridge Bank, Queenston, U.C., 1836-1841
The Northern Bank, Winnpeg, Man., 1905-1908

ne Northern Crown Bank, Winnipeg, Man., 1908-1918
ne Bank of Nova Scotia, Halifax, N.S., 1832 to date
ne Ontario Bank, Bowmanville, C.W., 1857-1906
ne Bank of Ottawa, Montreal, L.C., 1837
ne Bank of Ottawa, Ont., 1874-1919
ne Bank of the People, Toronto, U.C., 1835-1841
a Banque du Peuple, Montreal, L.C., 1835-1895
ne People's Bank of Halifax, Halifax, N.S., 1864-1905
ne People's Bank of New Brunswick, Fredericton, N.B., 1864-1907
ne Phenix Bank, Phillipsburg, L.C., 1837-1841
ne Pictou Bank, Pictou, N.S., 1873-1887
ne Bank of Prince Edward Island, Charlottetonwn, P.E.I., 1856-1881
ne Provincial Bank, London, Ont., 1884
ne Provincial Bank of Canada, Stanstead, Ont., 1856-1863
a Banque Provinciale du Canada, Montreal, Que., 1900-1979
ne Quebec Bank, Quebec, L.C., 1818-1917
ank of Quebec Lower Canada, Quebec, L.C., 1841
ne Royal Bank of Canada, Montreal, Que., 1901 to date
ne Royal Canadian Bank, Toronto, C.W., 1864-1876
ne Saint Francis Bank, Stanstead, C.E., 1855
. Banque de St. Hyacinthe St. Hyacinthe, Que., 1873-1908
. Banque de St. Jean, St. Jean, Que., 1873-1908
anque St. Jean Baptiste, Montreal, Que., 1875
ne St. Lawrence Bank, Toronto, Ont., 1872-1876
ne St. Lawrence Bank & Lumber Co., Malbaie, L.C., 1837
ne St. Stephen's Bank, St. Stephen, N.B., 1836-1910
ne Bank of Saskatchewan, Moose Jaw, Sask., 1913
ne Sovereign Bank of Canada, Montreal, Que., 1901-1908
ne Stadacona Bank, Quebec City, Que., 1872-1879
ne Standard Bank of Canada, Toronto,Ont., 1876-1928
ne Sterling Bank of Canada, Toronto, Ont., 1905-1924
ne Summerside Bank, Summerside, P.E.I., 1866-1901
attersall Bank, Montreal, L.C., 183-
ne Bank of Toronto, Toronto, Ont., 1855-1954
ne Traders Bank of Canada, Toronto, Ont., 1885-1912
ne Union Bank, Montreal, L.C., 1838-c.1840
ne Union Bank of Canada, Quebec City, Que., 1886-1925
1e Union Bank of Halifax, Halifax, N.S., 1856-1910
ne Union Bank of Lower Canada, Quebec, C.E., 1865-1886
ne Union Bank of Montreal, Montreal, L.C., c.1840
aion Bank of Newfoundland, St. John's, Nfld., 1854-1894
ne Union Bank of Prince Edward Island, Charlottetown, P.E.I., 1860-1893
aite Empire Bank of Canada, Toronto,Ont., 1906-1911
ank of Upper Canada, Kingston, U.C., 1819-1822
ank of Upper Canada, York, U.C., 1821-1866
e Bank of Vancouver, Vancouver, B.C., 1910-1914
e Bank of Victoria, Victoria, U.C., 1836
 Banque Ville Marie, Montreal, Que., 1872-1899
e Bank of Western Canada, Clifton, C.W., 1859-1863
e Western Bank of Canada, Oshawa, Ont., 1882-1909
e Westmoreland Bank of New Brunswick, N.B., 1854-1867
e Weyburn Security Bank, Weyburn, Sask., 1910-1931
e Bank of Yarmouth, Yarmouth, N.S., 1859-1905
e Zimmerman Bank, Elgin., C.W., 1854-1859

COLONIAL COINS AND TOKENS

Canada has produced a great number of tokens of various kinds over the years. Toke
were used as a form of currency prior to the institution of the decimal currency system in 18
(Colonial issues are not all tokens, some being regal coins). After Confederation, other kin
of tokens appeared, such as those for services, transportation and advertising purposes.

The prices in this section are for tokens in VG (very good) or F (fine) condition. Higher pric
will be paid for rare issues or for tokens in VF (very fine) or better condition.

NEWFOUNDLAND TOKENS

Date and Description	Buying Price	Date and Description	Buyi Pr
Rutherford - St. John's	2.50	1858 Sailing Ship	85
Rutherford - Harbour Grace	2.50	1860 Fishery Rights	15
McAuslane	1,200.00		

PRINCE EDWARD ISLAND TOKENS

te and scription	Buying Price	Date and Description	Buying Price
ey Dollar Ring*	1,500.00	McCarthy Penny	750.00
ey Dollar Plug*	1,500.00	Sheaf of Wheat	200.00
Causland Penny	750.00	Speed The Plough	1.50

te: Forgeries exist and are worth considerably less.

Date and Description	Buying Price	Date and Description	Buying Price
Fisheries & Agriculture	2.00	Fisheries & Agriculture	2
Self Government 1855 Prince Edward's	2.00	Ships Colonies 1815 One Penny	6
Self Government 1855 Prince Edward	2.00	Ships Colonies 1815 Publick Accommodation	6
Self Government 1857	2.00	Ships Colonies	2

Note: Tokens must be VG (very good) or better, with no discolouration.

NOVA SCOTIA
SEMI-REGAL TOKENS

Date and Description	Buying Price	Date and Description	Buying Price
3 Halfpenny	.50	1840 Halfpenny	.50
3 Penny	1.00	1840 Penny	1.00
4 Halfpenny	.50	1843 Half Penny	.50
4 Penny	1.00	1843 Penny	1.00
2 Halfpenny	.50	1856 Halfpenny	.50
2 Penny	1.00	1856 Penny	1.00

Date and Description	Buying Price	Date and Description	Buying Price
Broke - Halifax	2.00	Hosterman & Etter 1815	2
Convenience of Trade	3.00	Starr & Shannon	1
Carritt & Alport	3.00	Commercial Change	1
Hosterman & Etter	2.00	Miles W. White	1

NOVA SCOTIA
PRIVATE TOKENS

te and scription	Buying Price	Date and Description	Buying Price
n Alexr Barry	1.00	Trade & Navigation 1812	1.00
ifax Nova Scotia	2.00	Trade & Navigation 1813	15.00
A. & S. Black's	2.00	Pure Copper Preferable	1.00
Brown	1.00	Success to Navigation	1.00
L. White's	15.00	N.S & N.B. Success	15.00

Date and Description	Buying Price
1843 Halfpenny	.50
1843 Penny	.75
1854 Halfpenny	.50
1854 Penny	.75

Date and Description	Buying Price
McDermott	300
St. John	2
St. John's	1,750

LOWER CANADA TOKENS

te and scription	Buying Price	Date and Description	Buying Price
gdalen Island	10.00	Pro Bono Publico	1,500.00
k Token	1.00	Bank Token Halfpenny	.75
que du Peuple, Maple Leaf	1.00	Bank Token Penny	1.00
que du Peuple, Wreath	1.00	Bank of Montreal, Sideview Halfpenny	275.00
		Sideview Penny	475.00

Date and Description	Buying Price	Date and Description	Buying Price
Montreal Half Penny	2.00	Francis Mullins & Son	3
Canada Half Penny	2.00	R.W. Owen	1,500
For Public Accommodation	2.00	J. Shaw & Co.	3
T.S. Brown & Co.	2.00	J. Roy	15
Ths & Wm Molson	150.00	Agriculture & Commerce	

e and scription	Buying Price	Date and Description	Buying Price
fpenny Token 1812, Small Wreath	1.00	To Facilitate Trade	
fpenny Token 1812, Large Wreath	1.00	Military Bust 1825	2.00
ny Token 1812	2.00	Civilian Bust 1825	600.00
toria Nobis Est	2.00	Spread Eagle	1.00
Half Penny	2.00	Halfpenny Token	2.00

LOWER CANADA TOKENS

Date and Description	Buying Price	Date and Description	Buying Price
Seated Justice	1.00	Commercial Change	2
Bust/Ships Colonies	1.00	Bust and Harp	1

WELLINGTON TOKENS

Date and Description	Buying Price	Date and Description	Buying Price
Field Marshal Wellington	1.00	The Illustrious Wellington	1
Marquis Wellington	2.00	Battle Token	1

UPPER CANADA TOKENS

e and cription	Buying Price
ber Company	175.00
lie Halfpenny	3.00
lie Twopenny	35.00
abour No Bread	.75
saac Brock	.75

Date and Description	Buying Price
Success To Commerce	1.00
Upper & Lower Canada	15.00
Commercial Change 1815	10.00
Commerical Change 1820	1.00

UPPER CANADA TOKENS

Date and Description	Buying Price	Date and Description	Buying P
Commercial Change 1821		To Facilitate Trade	
Cask Marked Upper Canada	10.00	1823	
Cask Marked Jamaica	200.00	1833	
Province of Upper Canada	5.00	Commercial Change 1833	

PROVINCE OF CANADA TOKENS

PROVINCE OF CANADA TOKENS

e and cription	Buying Price
k of Montreal	
42, 1844 Halfpenny	.50
45 Halfpenny	1,000.00
37 Penny	50.00
42 Penny	1.00

Date and Description	Buying Price
Quebec Bank, 1852 Halfpenny	.50
Penny	1.00
Bank of Upper Canada 1850-1857	
Halfpenny	.50
Penny	1.00

ANONYMOUS AND MISCELLANEOUS TOKENS

e and cription	Buying Price
ieneral Accommodation	1.00
ess to Trade	10.00

Date and Description	Buying Price
Pure Copper Preferable	1.00
North American	10.00

BRITISH COLUMBIA TOKENS

TRANSPORTATION TOKENS

Date and Description	Buying Price
1802 Pattern Gold $10	25,000.00
1802 Pattern Gold $20	25,000.00

NORTH WEST COMPANY

Date and Description	Buying Price
1820 North West Company Token	300.00

HUDSON'S BAY COMPANY

Date and Description	Buying Price
Bridge Tokens, each	5
Montreal & Lachine Railroad	2

Date and Description	Buying Price
Hudson's Bay Company Tokens Set of four (1, ½, ¼, 1/8)	45.00

CANADIAN MEDALS

WAR MEDALS 1812 TO 1885

Army
Gold
Cross

Naval
General
Service
Medal

Army
Gold
Medal

Canadian
General
Service
Medal

Army
General
Service
Medal

Egyptian
Medal

Date and Description	Buying Price	Date and Description	Buying Price
Gold Cross	15,000.00	Canadian General Service Medal	
Gold Medal	5,000.00	Fenian Raid Bar 1866	125.00
General Service Medal 1812-1814		Fenian Raid Bar 1870	125.00
rt Detroit Bar	1,750.00	Red River Bar 1870	500.00
ateauguay Bar	1,750.00	Egyptian Medal*	
rysler's Farm Bar	1,750.00	The Nile Bar	500.00
al General Service Medal 1812-1814	150.00	Kirbekan Bar	500.00
		*Awarded to Canadian Boatmen	

WAR MEDALS 1885 TO 1914

Khedive's
Bronze
Star

1914
Star

North West
Canada
Medal

1914-1915
Star

South
Africa
Medal

British
War
Medal

Date and Description	Buying Price
Khedive's Bronze Star	15.00
North West Canada Medal 1885	150.00
Saskatchewan Bar	200.00
Queen's South Africa	
1899-1900 on reverse	1,750.00
Dates removed	20.00
King's South Africa	20.00

Date and Description	Buy P
1914 Star*	75
1914-1915 Star	
British War Medal	

*Canadian Star awarded only to 2nd. F Hospital.

WAR MEDALS 1914 TO 1945

Allied
Victory
Medal

The
Defence
Medal

Merchantile
Marine
War
Medal

WW II
1939-1945
War
Medal

Canadian
Volunteer
Service
Medal

Atlantic
Air Crew
Europe
Africa
France and
Germany
Italy
Pacific
Burma

e and cription	Buying Price
d Victory Medal	2.00
hantile Marine War Medal	5.00
adian Volunteer Service Medal	8.00
nce Medal	8.00
-1945 War Medal	8.00

Date and Description	Buying Price
1939-1945 Star	2.00
Atlantic Star	10.00
Air Crew Europe	50.00
Africa Star	2.00
France and Germany Star	2.00
Italy Star	2.00
Pacific Star	6.00
Burma Star	6.00

Canadian
Korean
Medal

1911
Coronation
Medal

United
Nations
Korea
Medal

1935
Silver
Jubilee
Medal

United
Nations
Emergency
Medal

1937
Coronation
Medal

Date and Description	Buying Price	Date and Description	Bu P
Canadian Korean War Medal, English	20.00	King George V	
Canadian Korean War Medal, French	30.00	Coronation Medal - 1911	1
United Nations Korea Medal	10.00	Silver Jubilee Medal - 1935	1
United Nations Emergency Medal	10.00	King George VI	
United Nations Medal 1960 to present	10.00	Coronation Medal - 1937	1
International Commission Medal 1967	10.00		
International Commission Medal 1973	10.00		

COMMEMORATIVE MEDALS

MEDALS FOR VALOUR AND SERVICE

1953
Coronation
Medal

Victoria
Cross

1977
Silver
Jubilee
Medal

Distinguished
Service
Order

1967
Canadian
Centennial
Medal

Order of
St. Michael
and
St. George

and cription	Buying Price	Date and Description	Buying Price
en Elizabeth II		Victoria Cross	25,000.00
onation Medal - 1953	10.00	Distinguished Service Order	200.00
er Jubilee Medal - 1977	35.00	Order of St. Michael and St. George	200.00
dian Centennial Medal - 1967	25.00		

MEDALS FOR VALOUR AND SERVICE

Distinguished
Service
Cross

Air
Force
Medal

Distinguished
Flying
Cross

Military
Medal

Air Force
Cross

British
Empire
Medal

Date and Description	Buying Price	Date and Description	Buy P
Distinguished Service Cross	200.00	Air Force Medal	10
Distinguished Flying Cross	300.00	Military Medal	15
Air Force Cross	350.00	British Empire Medal	5

COINS OF THE UNITED STATES

MINT MARKS

The United State decimal coinage is identified by the following mint marks:

C   -Charlotte, North Carolina
CC -Carson City, Nevada
D   -Dahlonega, Georgia (gold coins only)
D   -Denver, Colorado (1906 to date)
O   -New Orleans, Louisiana
S   -San Francisco, California
P   -Philadelphia, Pennsylvania

HALF CENTS

Liberty Cap

Date and Mint Mark	Buying Price
	750.00
	125.00
	100.00
	3,500.00
	150.00

Draped Bust

Date and Mint Mark	Buying Price
	20.00
	300.00
-1808	20.00

Classic Head

Date and Mint Mark	Buying Price
1809-1810	15.00
1811	75.00
1825 to 1835	12.50

Coronet Head

Date and Mint Mark	Buying Price
1849 to 1857	20.00

IMPORTANT NOTICE:
Buying prices are for coins in VG condition.

LARGE CENTS

Flowing Hair

Date and Mint Mark	Buying Price
1793 Wreath	750.00

Liberty Cap

Date and Mint Mark	Buying Price
1793	1,200.00
1794	100.00
1795	50.00
1796	75.00

Draped Bust

Date and Mint Mark	Buying Price
1796	55.00
1797	25.00
1798	20.00
1799	600.00
1800 to 1803	15.00
1804	250.00
1805 to 1807	12.50

Classic Head

Date and Mint Mark	Buying Price
1808	1
1809	40
1810	1
1811	30
1812 to 1814	1

Coronet Head

Date and Mint Mark	Buying Price
1816 to 1820	
1821	1
1822	
1823	20
1824 to 1838	
1839 to 1856	
1857	1

SMALL CENTS

Flying Eagle

Date and Mint Mark	Buying Price
1856	1,50
1857 to 1858	
1859	

Indian Head

e and t Mark	Buying Price
0 to 1864	2.00
5 to 1866	1.50
7 to 1872	14.00
3 to 1876	4.00
7	200.00
3	10.00
9 to 1886	.75
7 to 1908	.40
3S	15.00
9	.50
9S	125.00

Lincoln Head
Wheat Ears

e and t Mark	Buying Price
3	.10
VDB	.50
S	15.00
S VDB	150.00
to 1914	.10
D	35.00
D to 1931D	.10
S	14.00
to 1958	.01
Double Die	150.00

Lincoln Head Memorial

e and Mark	Buying Price
to 2001	.01

TWO CENTS

Date and Mint Mark	Buying Price
1864 to 1871	3.00
1872	25.00
1873 Proof	500.00

THREE CENTS

Silver

Date and Mint Mark	Buying Price
1851 to 1862	6.00
1863 to 1873 Proof	60.00

Nickel

Date and Mint Mark	Buying Price
1865 to 1874	4.00
1875 to 1876	5.00
1877 to 1878 Proof	250.00
1879 to 1880	25.00
1881	4.00
1882	30.00
1883	65.00
1884 to 1887	150.00
1888 to 1889	25.00

FIVE CENTS NICKEL

Shield

Date and Mint Mark	Buying Price
1866 to 1870	4.00
1871	12.00
1872 to 1878	5.00
1879 to 1881	80.00
1882 to 1883	4.00

Liberty Head

Date and Mint Mark	Buying Price
1883 to 1884	2.00
1885	85.00
1886	35.00
1887 to 1896	1.00
1897 to 1912D	.50
1912S	25.00

Indian Head or Buffalo Type

Date and Mint Mark	Buying Price
1913	2.00
1914 to 1918	.50
1918D 8/7	150.00
1919 to 1938	.25

Jefferson Type

Date and Mint Mark	Buying Price
1938 to 2001	

HALF DIMES

Flowing Hair

Date and Mint Mark	Buying Price
1794	300
1795	250

Draped Bust

Date and Mint Mark	Buying Price
1796 to 1797	350
1800 to 1801	200
1802	3,500
1803 to 1805	175

Capped Bust

Date and Mint Mark	Buying Price
1829 to 1837	

Liberty Seated

Date and Mint Mark	Buying Price
37	12.00
38 No Stars	30.00
38 to 1845	3.50
46	50.00
47 to 1863	4.00
64	90.00
64S	12.00
65	75.00
66	75.00
66S	8.00
67	125.00
67S	8.00
68 to 1873	3.50

DIMES

Draped Bust

Date and Mint Mark	Buying Price
96 to 1797	500.00
98 to 1807	200.00

Capped Bust

Date and Mint Mark	Buying Price
9 to 1811	30.00
4 to 1821	8.00
2	150.00
3 to 1837	8.00

Liberty Seated

Date and Mint Mark	Buying Price
1837 to 1838 No stars	20.00
1839 to 1840O	3.00
1840	15.00
1841 to 1843	3.00
1843O and 1844	20.00
1845	2.00
1846	25.00
1847 to 1856	3.00
1856S	25.00
1857 to 1860	3.00
1858S	25.00
1859S	45.00
1860O	200.00
1861 and 1862	4.00
1863	75.00
1864 to 1867	75.00
1864S to 1867S	6.00
1868 to 1874	4.00
1871CC	300.00
1872CC	150.00
1873CC No Arrows	Unique
1874CC	150.00
1875 to 1878	2.00
1878CC	2.50
1879	80.00
1880 to 1881	45.00
1882 to 1885	3.00
1885S	150.00
1886 to 1891	3.00

Barber

Date and Mint Mark	Buying Price
1892 to 1895	1.50
1895O	200.00
1896O	40.00
1897 to 1916	.40

111

Mercury Head

Date and Mint Mark	Buying Price
1916	.45
1916D	250.00
1917 to 1945	.45

Roosevelt - Silver

Date and Mint Mark	Buying Price
1946 to 1964	.45

Roosevelt - Clad

Date and Mint Mark	Buying Price
1965 to 2001	.10

TWENTY CENTS

Date and Mint Mark	Buying Price
1875 to 1876	30.00
1877 to 1878	250.00

QUARTER DOLLAR

Draped Bust

Date and Mint Mark	Buying Price
1796	2,500.
1804	600.
1805 to 1807	100.

Capped Bust

Date and Mint Mark	Buying Price
1815 to 1822	25
1823/2	3,500
1824 to 1828	20
1831 to 1838 Reduced Size	20

Liberty Seated

Date and Mint Mark	Buying Price
1838 to 1849	6
1849O	200
1850 to 1851	15
1851O	100
1852	20
1852O	85

te and nt Mark	Buying Price
3 to 1862	5.00
2S to 1864	10.00
4S	85.00
5 to 1870	20.00
0CC	600.00
1CC	500.00
1S	100.00
2CC	150.00
2S	100.00
1 to 1878CC	4.00
8S to 1888	35.00
8S	4.00
9 and 1890	25.00
10	45.00
1 and 1891S	4.00

Barber

te and nt Mark	Buying Price
2 to 1896	1.00
6S	125.00
7 to 1901	1.00
1S	750.00
2 to 1913	1.00
3S	200.00
4 to 1916	1.00

Standing Liberty

te and nt Mark	Buying Price
6	500.00
7 to 1930	1.00

Washington - Silver

Date and Mint Mark	Buying Price
1932 to 1964	1.00

Washington - Clad

Date and Mint Mark	Buying Price
1965 to 1975	.25

200th Bi-Centennial

Date and Mint Mark	Buying Price
1976	.25

Washington - Clad

Date and Mint Mark	Buying Price
1977 to 2000	.25

Note: Coins must be in very good condition or better to command these prices, coins grading good or less will sell at lower prices.

HALF DOLLARS
Flowing Hair

Date and Mint Mark	Buying Price
1794	700.00
1795	200.00

Draped Bust

Date and Mint Mark	Buying Price
1796 15 Stars	4,000.00
1796 16 Stars	4,000.00
1797 15 Stars	4,000.00
1801 to 1802	75.00
1803 to 1807	40.00

Capped Bust

Date and Mint Mark	Buying Price
1807	25.00
1808 to 1814	15.00

Date and Mint Mark	Buying Price
1815	350
1817 to 1836	20
1836 Reeded Edge	300
1837 to 1839	20
1839O	65

Liberty Seated

Date and Mint Mark	Buying Price
1839 to 1852O	10
1850	50
1851	60
1852	80
1853O	10,000
1853 to 1855	10
1855S Arrows	150
1856 to 1865S	8
1866 to 1873CC	6
1870CC	200
1873 to 1874S	15
1875 to 1878	6
1878CC	125
1878S	2,000
1879 to 1890	50
1891	8

Barber

Date and Mint Mark	Buying Price
1892	9
1892O and 1892S	50
1893 to 1897	3
1897O	20
1897S	35
1898 to 1915	2

Liberty Walking

Date and Mint Mark	Buying Price
16 to 1920	2.00
1	25.00
1D	40.00
3 to 1947	2.00

Franklin

Date and Mint Mark	Buying Price
8 to 1963	2.00

Kennedy - Silver

Date and Mint Mark	Buying Price
4	2.00

Kennedy - Silver Clad

Date and Mint Mark	Buying Price
5 to 1970	1.00

Kennedy - Copper Clad

Date and Mint Mark	Buying Price
1971 to 1998	.50

SILVER DOLLARS

Flowing Hair

Date and Mint Mark	Buying Price
1794	4,000.00
1795	350.00

Draped Bust

Date and Mint Mark	Buying Price
1795	300.00
1796 to 1798	300.00
1798 to 1803	125.00

Note: Coins must grade very good (VG) or better to command prices listed.

Liberty Seated

Date and Mint Mark	Buying Price
1840 to 1873	35.00
1851 and 1852	1,000.00
1858	800.00
1870CC	100.00
1870S	20,000.00
1871CC	750.00
1872CC	300.00
1872S	75.00
1873CC	900.00

Liberty Head

Date and Mint Mark	Buying Price
1878 to 1892	5.00
1878CC to 1881CC	13.00
1882CC to 1884CC	15.00
1885CC	75.00
1889CC	125.00
1893CC	125.00
1890O to 1893O	5.00
1893S	500.00
1894	100.00
1895O	65.00
1895S	80.00
1896 to 1903	5.00
1903O	50.00
1904 to 1921	5.00

Peace

Date and Mint Mark	Buying Price
1921 to 1927	5
1928	35
1928S to 1935	5

Eisenhower

Date and Mint Mark	Buying Price
1971 to 1976	1

Susan B. Anthony

Date and Mint Mark	Buying Price
1979 to 1981	1

TRADE DOLLARS

Date and Mint Mark	Buying Price
₹3 to 1878	25.00
₹8CC	75.00

GOLD DOLLARS

Type 1 Liberty Head

Date and Mint Mark	Buying Price
49 to 1854	75.00

Type 2 Indian Head, Small

Date and Mint Mark	Buying Price
54 to 1855	100.00
55C	400.00
55D	800.00

Type 3 Indian Head, Large

Date and Mint Mark	Buying Price
1856 to 1889	75.00
1856D	600.00
1860D	500.00
1861D	1,200.00
1875	450.00

GOLD 2 ½ DOLLARS

Capped Bust Right

Date and Mint Mark	Buying Price
1796	2,000.00
1797 to 1807	600.00

Capped Bust Left

Date and Mint Mark	Buying Price
1808	2,000.00

Capped Head Left

Date and Mint Mark	Buying Price
1821 to 1827	700.00
1829 to 1833	600.00
1834 (motto)	1,500.00

Classic Head

Date and Mint Mark	Buying Price
1834 to 1839	125.00

Coronet Head

Date and Mint Mark	Buying Price
1840 to 1907	90.00
1848 California	2,000.00
1854D	500.00
1854S	12,500.00
1855D	350.00
1856D	450.00
1875	250.00

Indian Head

Date and Mint Mark	Buying Price
1908 to 1929	90.00
1911D	150.00

3 DOLLARS

Date and Mint Mark	Buying Price
1854 to 1873	275.00
1854D	900.00
1873 Closed 3	800.00
1880 to 1889	275.00

4 DOLLARS

Date and Mint Mark	Buying Price
1879 to 1880	6,000.

GOLD 5 DOLLARS

Capped Bust Right

Date and Mint Mark	Buying Price
1795 to 1797	2,000.
1798 to 1807	500.

Draped Bust Left

Date and Mint Mark	Buying Price
1807 to 1834	800.0
1821	700.0
1822	55,000.0
1823	500.0
1824	1,000.0
1825	1,000.0
1826	800.0
1827	1,250.0
1828	1,500.0
1829	1,500.0

Classic Head

Date and Mint Mark	Buying Price
1834 to 1838	100.00
1838C	300.00
1838D	300.00

Coronet Head

Date and Mint Mark	Buying Price
1839 to 1908	100.00
1842C Small Date	350.00
1854S	30,000.00
1861C	300.00
1861D	600.00
1864S	175.00
1865	150.00
1870CC	250.00
1875	5,000.00
1878CC	250.00

Indian Head

Date and Mint Mark	Buying Price
1908 to 1916	115.00
1929	500.00

GOLD 10 DOLLARS

Capped Bust Right

Date and Mint Mark	Buying Price
Small Eagle, 1795 to 1797	1,500.00
Heraldic Eagle, 1797 to 1803	600.00

Coronet Head

Date and Mint Mark	Buying Price
1838 to 1907	200.00
1858	400.00
1859O	250.00
1859S	250.00
1863	400.00
1864S	500.00
1865S	275.00
1866S	275.00
1870CC	500.00
1873	300.00
1873CC	250.00
1875 Proof	5,000.00
1876	300.00
1877	300.00
1877CC	300.00
1878CC	300.00
1879CC	500.00
1879O	250.00
1883O	275.00

$10 Indian Head

Date and Mint Mark	Buying Price
1907 to 1932	250.00
1920S	500.00
1930S	400.00
1933	5,000.00

GOLD $20 DOLLARS

Liberty

Date and Mint Mark	Buying Price
1850 to 1907	400.00
1854O	3,000.00
1855O	600.00
1856O	3,500.00
1859O	650.00
1860O	650.00
1861O	450.00
1870CC	5,000.00
1871CC	500.00
1879O	500.00
1881	550.00
1882	700.00
1885	650.00
1886	650.00
1891	500.00
1891CC	450.00

$20 St. Gaudens

Date and Mint Mark	Buying Price
1907 MCMVII	800.
1907 to 1916	400.
1920S	1,000.
1921	1,100.
1922 to 1928	400.
1927D	15,000.
1927S	600.
1929	750.
1930 to 1932	1,500.

GOLD COMMEMORATIVE COINS

Date and Mint Mark	Buying Price
1903 $1 Louisiana Purchase	150.
1904-05 $1 Lewis & Clark Exposition	200.
1915S $1 Panama-Pacific Exposition	150.
1916 $1 McKinley Memorial	150.
1917 $1 McKinley Memorial	175.
1922 $1 Grant Memorial, With Star	450.
1922 $1 Grant Memorial, Without Star	400.
1915S $2.50 Panama-Pacific Exposition	500.
1926 $2.50 Philadelphia Sesquicentennial	100.
1984P and D $10 Olympic	200.
1984S $10 Olympic	200.
1984W $10 Olympic	200.
1986W $5 Liberty	100.
1987W $5 Constitution	100.
1988W $5 Oylmpic	100.
1989W $5 Congress	100.
1991W $5 Mount Rushmore	100.
1992W $5 Olympic	100.
1992W $5 Columbus	100.
1993W $5 Bill of Rights	100.
1993W $5 WWII	100.
1994W $5 World Cup	100.
1995 W $5 Civil War	100.
1995W $5 Olympic Torch	100.
1995W $5 Olympic Stadium	100.
1996W $5 Flag Bearer	100.
1996W $5 Cauldron	100.
1996W $5 Smithsonian	100.
1997W $5 F.D.R.	100.

WORLD GOLD COINS

his partial listing of world gold coins indicates the prices dealers are willing to pay based on
e Canadian dollar gold price as at August 6th, 2000. Prices will fluctuate with the market
ice of gold, plus the Canadian-U.S. dollar exchange rate.

AUSTRIA

ate and nom.	Fine Gold Content Oz.	Buying Price
12 10K	0.0980	32.50
15 20K	0.1960	65.00
15 100K	0.9803	325.00
15 1D	0.1109	37.00
14 4D	0.4438	147.00
92 10Fr	0.0933	31.00
92 20Fr*	0.1867	62.00

BAHAMAS

ate and nom.	Fine Gold Content Oz.	Buying Price
67 $10	0.1177	39.00
71 $10	0.1177	39.00
72 $10	0.0940	32.00
67 $20	0.2355	78.00
71 $20*	0.2355	78.00
72 $20	0.1880	62.00
67 $50	0.5888	195.00
71 $50	0.5888	195.00
72 $50	0.4708	156.00
67 $100	1.1776	390.00
71 $100	1.1776	390.00
72 $100	0.9420	312.00

Coin illustrated

BELGIUM

Date and Denom.	Fine Gold Content Oz.	Buying Price
1867 to 1914 20Fr	0.1867	62.00

BERMUDA

Date and Denom.	Fine Gold Content Oz.	Buying Price
1970 $20	0.2355	78.00
1977 $50	0.1172	39.00
1975 $100*	0.2304	76.00
1977 $100	0.2344	76.00

CAYMAN ISLANDS

Date and Denom.	Fine Gold Content Oz.	Buying Price
1972 $25*	0.2532	84.00
1974 $50	0.1823	60.00
1974 $100	0.3646	121.00
1975 $100	0.3646	121.00
1977 $100	0.3464	115.00

CHILE

Date and Denom.	Fine Gold Content Oz.	Buying Price
1898 to 1900 5p	0.0883	29.00
1896 to 1901 10p*	0.1766	58.00
1896 to 1917 20p	0.3532	116.00
1926 to 1980 100p	0.5886	195.00

COLUMBIA

Date and Denom.	Fine Gold Content Oz.	Buying Price
1913 to 1929 2 ½ p	0.1177	39.00
1913 to 1930 5p	0.2355	78.00
1919 and 1924 10p	0.4710	156.00
1973 1500p*	0.5527	183.00

FRANCE

Date and Denom.	Fine Gold Content Oz.	Buying Price
1856 to 1869 5Fr	0.0467	16.00
1854 to 1914 10Fr	0.0933	31.00
1809 to 1914 20Fr*	0.1867	62.00
1810 to 1838 40Fr	0.3734	125.00
1855 to 1864 50Fr	0.4667	155.00
1855 to 1913 100Fr	0.9335	330.00

GERMANY

Date and Denom.	Fine Gold Content Oz.	Buying Price
1872 to 1914 10DM	0.1152	38.
1871 to 1914 20DM*	0.2304	76.

GREAT BRITAIN

Date and Denom.	Fine Gold Content Oz.	Buying Pr
1863 to 1915 ½ Sov.	0.1177	39.0
1871 to 1968 Sov.*	0.2354	78.
1887 Two Pound	0.4708	156.
1897 Two Pound	0.4708	156.
1902 Two Pound	0.4708	156.
1911 Two Pound	0.4708	156.
1937 Two Pound	0.4708	156
1887 Five Pound	1.1773	390.
1897 Five Pound	1.1773	390.
1902 Five Pound	1.1773	390.
1911 Five Pound	1.1773	390.
1937 Five Pound	1.1773	390.

IRAN

Date and Denom.	Fine Gold Content Oz.	Buyin Pri
1971 500R	0.1883	62.
1971 750R*	0.2827	94.
1971 1000R	0.3770	125.
1971 2000R	0.7541	250.

* Coin illustrated

ITALY

Date and nom.	Fine Gold Content Oz.	Buying Price
32 to 1860 10L	0.0931	31.00
31 to 1860 20L*	0.1867	62.00
22 to 1831 40L	0.3733	124.00
32 to 1844 100L	0.9332	309.00

JAMAICA

Date and nom.	Fine Gold Content Oz.	Buying Price
72 $20*	0.2531	84.00
75, 1976 $100	0.2265	75.00
78 $100	0.3281	109.00
78, 1979 $250	1.2507	415.00

MEXICO

Date and nom.	Fine Gold Content Oz.	Buying Price
45 2p	0.0482	17.00
45 2 1/2p	0.0602	21.00
55 5p	0.1205	43.00
59 10p*	0.2411	86.00
59 20p	0.4823	172.00
47 50p	1.2057	430.00

ove dates are restrikes.

Coin Illustrated

NETHERLANDS

Date and Denom.	Fine Gold Content Oz.	Buying Price
1900 to 1937 1D*	0.1109	37.00
1912 5G	0.0973	32.00
1875 to 1933 10G	0.1947	65.00

PANAMA

Date and Denom.	Fine Gold Content Oz.	Buying Price
1975 to 1979 100B*	0.2361	78.00
1975 to 1979 500B	1.2067	400.00

RUSSIA

Date and Denom.	Fine Gold Content Oz.	Buying Price
1897 to 1911 5R*	0.1244	41.00
1897 7 1/2R	0.1867	62.00
1898 to 1911 10R	0.2489	82.00
1897 15R	0.3734	124.00
1977 to 1988 100R	0.5000	165.00

IMPORTANT: Buying prices are listed for coins graded VF or better. Bent, damaged or badly worn coins are worth less.

APPENDIX

BULLION VALUES

Silver and gold coins and other numismatic items are often bought by dealers for their bulli value, that is the value of the pure precious metals which they contain. The weight of precic metals is expressed in grams or troy ounces, not in avoirdupois ounces. A troy ounce is grea than an avoirdupois ounce.

1 Troy Ounce = 31.21035 Grams
1 Avoirdupois Ounce = 28.349 Grams

GOLD

The quantity of pure gold in gold coins is calculated by multiplying the gold fineness or pur of the coin by its weight in troy ounces or grams. Gold purity can also be expressed in kara a 24-part system with 24-karats equalling pure gold, 22 karats equalling 22 parts gold to parts base metal, 18 karats equalling 18 parts gold to 6 parts base metal etc.

Karats	Fineness	Purity
24	.999	99.9%
22	.916	91.6%
18	.750	75.0%
14	.585	58.5%
10	.417	41.7%
9	.375	37.5%

1 14-karat or .585 fine gold coin weighing 1 troy ounce contains 1 ounce x .585 = .585 tr ounces of pure gold. If gold is worth $600 per troy ounce, then this coin is worth $600 x .5 = $351. (See extended charts on following pages.)

SILVER

The quantity of pure silver in silver coins is calculated by multiplying the silver fineness or pur of the coin by its weight in troy ounces.

Karats	Fineness	Purity
Pure	.999	99.9%
Fine	.999	99.9%
Sterling	.925	92.5%
Coin	.800	80.0%
Coin	.500	50.0%

A .800 fine silver coin weighing 1 troy ounce contains 1 x .800 = .800 troy ounces of pu silver. If silver is worth $20 an ounce, then this coin is worth $20 x .800 = $16. (See extend charts on following pages.)

GOLD CONTENT OF CANADIAN GOLD COIN

nom.	Date and Mint Mark	Gross Weight (Grams)	Fineness	Pure Gold Content Grams	Troy Oz.
d.	1908C-1910C	7.99	.917	7.32	.236
d.	1911C-1919C	7.99	.917	7.32	.236
	1865-1888	3.33	.917	3.05	.100
	1912-1914	8.36	.900	7.52	.242
0	1912-1914	16.72	.900	15.05	.484
0	1967	18.27	.900	16.45	.529
M.L.	1982 to date	3.11	.9999	3.11	.10
0 M.L.	1982 to date	7.78	.9999	7.78	.25
0 M.L.	1986 to date	15.57	.9999	15.57	.500
0 M.L.	1979 to date	31.10	.999	31.10	1.000
00	1976 (Unc.)	13.33	.583	7.78	.250
00	1976 (Proof)	16.96	.917	15.55	.499
00	1977-1986	16.96	.917	15.55	.499
00	1987 to date	13.33	.583	7.78	.250
75	1992	16.97	.916	15.544	.500
00	1990 to date	17.106	.916	15.669	.500
50	1998 to date	38.05	.9999	38.050	1.223

SILVER CONTENT OF CANADIAN SILVER COINS

nom.	Date	Fineness	Silver Content Grams	Troy Oz.
0	1985-1988	.925	31.103	1.000
0	1973-1976	.925	44.955	1.445
	1973-1976	.925	22.477	.723
M.L.	1987 to date	.999	31.103	1.000
	1935-1967	.800	18.661	.600
	1971 to date	.500	11.662	.375
cents	1870-1919	.925	10.792	.347
cents	1920-1967	.800	9.330	.300
cents	1870-1919	.925	5.370	.173
cents	1920-1967	.800	4.665	.150
cents	1967-1968	.500	2.923	.094
cents	1858-1919	.925	2.146	.069
cents	1920-1967	.800	1.866	.060
cents	1967-1968	.500	1.170	.038
cents	1858-1919	.925	1.080	.034
cents	1920-1921	.800	.933	.030

PLATINUM CONTENT OF CANADIAN PLATINUM COINS

nom.	Date	Fineness	Platinum Content Grams	Troy Oz.
00	1990-2000	.9999	31.1	1.000
50	1990-2000	.9999	15.6	.500
5	1990-2000	.9999	7.8	.250
0	1990-2000	.9999	3.1	.100

BULLION VALUES OF CANADIAN GOLD COINS

Computed from $300 to $700 per troy ounce in increments of $100 Canadian.

Denom.	Date and Mint Mark	$300	$400	$500	$600	$7
1 pd.	1908C-1910C	70.95	94.40	118.00	141.60	165.
1 pd.	1911C-1919C	70.95	94.40	118.00	141.60	165.
$2	1865-1888	30.00	40.00	50.00	60.00	70
$5	1912-1914	72.60	96.60	121.00	145.20	160.
$10	1912-1914	145.20	193.60	242.00	290.40	338.
$20	1967	15.70	211.60	264.50	317.40	370
$5 M.L.	1982 to date	30.00	40.00	50.00	60.00	70.
$10 M.L.	1982 to date	75.00	100.00	125.00	150.00	175.
$20 M.L.	1986 to date	150.00	200.00	250.00	300.00	350.
$50 M.L.	1979 to date	300.00	400.00	500.00	600.00	700.
$100	1976 (Unc)	75.00	100.00	125.00	150.00	175
$100	1976 (Proof)	150.00	200.00	250.00	300.00	350.
$100	1977-1986	150.00	200.00	250.00	300.00	350.
$100	1987 (Proof)	75.00	100.00	125.00	150.00	175

BULLION VALUES OF CANADIAN SILVER COINS

Computed from $5 to $50 per troy ounce in increments of $10 Canadian.

Denom.	Fineness	$5	$10	$20	$30	$40	$
$20	.925	5.00	10.00	20.00	30.00	40.00	50.
$10	.925	7.23	14.00	28.90	43.35	57.80	72.
$5	.925	3.62	7.23	14.46	21.69	28.92	36.
$5 M.L.	.999	5.00	10.00	20.00	30.00	40.00	50.
$1	.800	3.00	6.00	12.00	18.00	24.00	30.
$1	.500	1.88	3.75	7.50	11.25	15.00	18.
50 cents	.925	1.74	3.47	6.94	10.41	13.88	17.
50 cents	.800	1.50	3.00	6.00	9.00	12.00	15.
25 cents	.925	.87	1.73	3.46	5.19	6.92	8.
25 cents	.800	.75	1.50	3.00	4.50	6.00	7.
25 cents	.500	.47	.94	1.88	2.82	3.76	4.
10 cents	.925	.35	.69	1.38	2.07	2.76	3.
10 cents	.800	.30	.60	1.20	1.80	2.40	3.
10 cents	.500	.19	.38	.76	1.14	1.52	1.
5 cents	.925	.17	.34	.68	1.02	1.36	1.
5-cents	.800	.15	.30	.60	.90	1.20	1.

Application for Membership/Subscription

Applications for membership/subscription in the Canadian Numismatic Association may be made by any reputable party upon payment of the required dues.

(check one of each group)

❏ New   ❏ Renewal _____   ❏ Reinstatement
                    (member number)
❏Regular   ❏Junior   ❏Family
❏Corporate   ❏Life Membership

❏Mr.   ❏Mrs.   ❏Ms.   ❏Club

Name:

Street: *Address may be published in the Journal ❏ yes ❏ no*

City: *Province/State*   *Postal Code/Zip*

Country   *Birthdate*

Signature of applicant   *Signature of Sponsor*

Signature of guardian (if under 18 years of age)

Dues

Dues shown are in Canadian dollars to Canadian addresses and in U.S. dollars to all other addresses. Payment may be made by money order, bank draft or personal cheque. We regret that we are unable to offer credit card services. Postage stamps are not acceptable. Currency (U.S. or Canadian only) is acceptable and should be sent by security registered mail only. Membership is not Goods and Services taxable.

REGULAR* - Applicants 18 years of age or over......................**$33.00**

JUNIOR - Applicants under 18 years of age **$16.50**
      Persons under 18 must be sponsored by a parent or guardian

FAMILY - Husband, wife and children at home, under 18 years of age
      One Journal only **$44.00**

CORPORATE - Clubs, Societies, Libraries and other non-profit
      organizations..**$33.00**

LIFE MEMBERSHIP **$495.00**

(After one year of regular membership. Details on payment plan available on request.)

First class mailing of the Journal is available on remittance of $9.00 (Cdn.) to Canadian addresses, $7.50 (U.S.$) to U.S.A. addresses and $15.00 (U.S.$) to all other addresses. Addresses of all new members are published in the Journal.

Please mail application and payment to the Canadian Numismatic Association, P.O. Box 226, Barrie, Ontario, Canada, L4M 4T2.
Application must be complete and accompanied by full dues to be accepted.
Please photocopy and mail.